News Media and the Indigenous Fight for Federal Recognition

To Devin,

Tell good stories!

CR

News Media and the Indigenous Fight for Federal Recognition

Cristina L. Azocar

LEXINGTON BOOKS
Lanham • Boulder • New York • London

Preface epigraph Smith Tuhiwai L., Decolonizing Methodologies, Red Talks, San Francisco State University. (Feb. 11, 2021). https://www.youtube.com/watch?v=bboxzss_PxM&feature=youtu.be accessed February 23, 2021.

Chapter 4 epigraph Kelly Casey R. "Orwellian Language and the Politics of Tribal Termination (1953–1960)." *Western Journal of Communication*, 74(4), (July 19, 2010). 351–371.

Chapter 6 epigraph Extracted from Luna-Firebaugh, Eileen M. and Mary Jo Tippeconnic Fox, 2010. "The Sharing Tradition Indian Gaming in Stories and Modern Life." *Wicazo Sa Review*, 25 (1) 75-86.

Chapter 9 epigraph Wilkinson, Gerald. "Colonialism Through the Media." *The Indian Historian*, 7(3) (1974). 6.

Published by Lexington Books
An imprint of The Rowman & Littlefield Publishing Group, Inc.
4501 Forbes Boulevard, Suite 200, Lanham, Maryland 20706
www.rowman.com

6 Tinworth Street, London SE11 5AL, United Kingdom

Copyright © 2022 The Rowman & Littlefield Publishing Group, Inc.

All rights reserved. No part of this book may be reproduced in any form or by any electronic or mechanical means, including information storage and retrieval systems, without written permission from the publisher, except by a reviewer who may quote passages in a review.

British Library Cataloguing in Publication Information Available

Library of Congress Cataloging-in-Publication Data

Names: Azocar, Cristina, author.
Title: News media and the indigenous fight for Federal recognition / Cristina Azocar.
Description: Lanham : Lexington Books, [2022] | Includes bibliographical references and index. | Summary: "Federal recognition enables tribes to govern themselves and make decisions for their citizens that have the power to retain their cultures. This book examines how news coverage has prioritized gaming over sovereignty and interfered in tribes' ability to be federally recognized" —Provided by publisher.
Identifiers: LCCN 2022004515 (print) | LCCN 2022004516 (ebook) | ISBN 9781793640390 (cloth) | ISBN 9781793640406 (epub)
Subjects: LCSH: Indians of North America—Press coverage. | Federally recognized Indian tribes—Press coverage. | Indians of North America—Legal status, laws, etc.—Press coverage. | Indians of North America—Gambling—Press coverage. | Indians of North America—Government relations—Press coverage.
Classification: LCC PN4888.I52 A96 2022 (print) | LCC PN4888.I52 (ebook) | DDC 070.4/4997000497—dc23/eng/20220224
LC record available at https://lccn.loc.gov/2022004515
LC ebook record available at https://lccn.loc.gov/2022004516

∞™ The paper used in this publication meets the minimum requirements of American National Standard for Information Sciences—Permanence of Paper for Printed Library Materials, ANSI/NISO Z39.48-1992.

Dedication

"Every single one of us is the legacy of our ancestors."
—Patty Talahongva, Hopi, Executive
Producer of *Indian Country Today*

For the women who made me who I am: my great grandmothers Mollie Adams and Alice Adams, my grandmother Mary Alice Adams, my sister Nicole Azocar, and especially my mom Nora Adams Azocar.

Figure 0.1 Image of Mollie Holmes Adams. Portrait of Mollie Holmes Adams circa 1918 courtesy of the National Museum of the American Indian, Smithsonian Institution (N12647). Photo By NMAI Photo Services.

Turkey Feather Mantel by Mollie Adams (Upper Mattaponi) courtesy of Jamestown-Yorktown Foundation Collection.

Porcupine Medicine Wheel courtesy of Roberta Shields (Navajo and Cheyenne River Lakota Sioux).

Contents

Preface		ix
Acknowledgments		xiii
1	Federal Recognition, Jim Crow, and the News Media	1
2	Who Is Indian and Who Decides?	13
3	Federal Recognition and White Supremacy	21
4	Hegemony, Framing, and Agenda Setting in Indian Country	37
5	Indigenous Standpoint Theory and News Coverage	51
6	History of News Coverage of Federal Recognition	57
7	Forty Years of News Coverage of Federal Recognition	63
8	Coverage of the Federal Recognition of Virginia Tribes	75
9	Indigenous News Coverage of Federal Recognition	87
10	Perspectives from Native Journalists and Legal Experts on Covering Federal Recognition: Indigenous Standpoint Theory in Action	95
11	Federal Recognition Does Not Equate to Casinos	107

12 Indigenous Standpoint Journalism for Non-Indigenous Journalists 113

Epilogue: A Final Story About Federal Recognition and COVID-19
and Casinos 117

Appendices 121

Bibliography 131

Index 149

About the Author 155

Preface

A STORY

"There are some common threads in Indigenous research and one of the more powerful ones would be storytelling . . . you can go across the world and [find in] different Indigenous contexts the power of storytelling, of telling our own stories."[1] —Linda Tuhiwai Smith

The following is a story to understand the content and context of this book.

CHIEF KENNETH ADAMS' STORY

This first story is based on an interview with Kenneth Adams, my uncle. In January 2001, he was elected chief of the Upper Mattaponi Tribe, and remained so for fifteen years. Kenny told me that the Tribe filed a Letter of Intent in 1979 to acquire federal recognition. However, it was not until 1999—when a group of tribal leaders got together to discuss petitioning for federal recognition through an Act of Congress—that the process really began in earnest. Virginia's Democratic Representative James Moran sponsored federal legislation for the recognition of the Upper Mattaponi. Democrats were in the minority in the House of Representatives (HoR) at that time, and issues relating to Tribes had to come up through the Interior, Environment, and Related Agencies Subcommittee of the House Committee on Appropriations, but the Republican chair of that committee was not interested in holding a hearing on this matter. Fortunately, there was a way to have the minority party hold an ad-hoc (and unofficial) hearing. Therefore, in late summer 2002, the Tribe decided to pursue this direction; then the Republican chair of the House Committee on Appropriations agreed to a hearing in September. Kenny testified at that hearing. Then he testified again, along with Chickahominy tribal Chief Stephen Adkins, the following month at the Senate's Indian Affairs Committee hearing. The Senate bill passed the committee, and thereafter went before the full Senate. But it stopped there.

Then, a new Congress was seated—and the process had to start from the beginning with a new bill. The Tribes then started the process over again every two years with a new Congress until a bill finally passed in 2018. But the bill had to include anti-gaming language in order for it to pass, even though none of the Tribes seeking recognition had gaming interests. The absurd argument made that led to this language was that maybe this generation of Indians were uninterested in gaming, but future members might be interested.

I asked my uncle about his relationship with the news media prior to the tribe's pursuit of federal recognition, and he said they did not really contact him much until the approaching 400th anniversary in 2007 of the Jamestown Settlement by the British. He could not recall specifically seeing any negative coverage, but this may have been because of the relationships he developed with some reporters—and because the tribal leaders organized press conferences about the federal recognition process in which they were able to lead the agenda.

Before the process of federal acknowledgment began, there was an issue of water use centering around a reservoir project. The Virginia Department of Historic Resources indicated to the Army Corps of Engineers that they would have to treat the Upper Mattaponi as if federally recognized[2]—even though this was not the case. The reporters at the time knew that the Tribe was seeking federal recognition, and Kenny told me that on that occasion he wished the news media would have covered the issue more than they did.

Achieving federal recognition was a long process that would wax and wane, and it took two decades. When Kenny first started talking to the media, he said he was hesitant. However, after a few years of talking to reporters, he became more confident and bolder in planning the news coverage and deciding the agenda for the press conferences.

Kenny said the entire recognition process was rough and very demanding of his time and energy—especially in raising money to pay lobbyists. When the first payment was due to the lobbyist, he told her (the lobbyist) that he had to get $78 from ten people to pay the $780 owed her toward lobbying the United States Congress for the federal recognition.

My uncle Kenny said, "I went over to Lou's [his sister, my aunt] and Mama was there. That was about six years before she passed. I was just sitting at the table talking. Then, my mama says, 'I'm gonna give you $20.' And I said, 'Mamma, you don't have to do that.' And she said, 'No, I want to do it.' And that was the first donation."

NOTES

1. Smith, 2021.
2. Dussias, 2011.

Acknowledgments

This book is the culmination of my long-standing frustration in reading mainstream news media accounts of the federal recognition process of U.S. Indigenous Tribes. I was first introduced to the issue of biased media coverage of people of color in the ethnic diversity and journalism class that I attended as a journalism student at San Francisco State University. Jon Funabiki (who later became the Media and Culture Program Officer at the Ford Foundation and then the Director of Renaissance Journalism) was my professor. At that time, the class was only a five-week course, so we did not have sufficient time to delve into all of the details of the centuries of harm inflicted on communities of color by the news media. Jon saw something in me (or possibly it was just that I was the only Native student in the class), and in 1993 asked me to be one of four student research assistants preparing a report for a convention of journalists of color in Atlanta, Georgia.

We presented *Newswatch: A Critical Look at Coverage of People of Color* at the first Unity Journalists of Color Conference in 1994. This was a gathering of more than 8,000 journalists representing the Asian American Journalists Association, the National Association of Hispanic Journalists, the National Association of Black Journalists, and the Native American Journalists Association (NAJA). I did not even know NAJA existed until then. Many of the Indigenous journalists I met at that conference almost thirty years ago continue to inspire me today. Loren Tapahe (Diné)—Native Scene publisher (and also one of the founders of NAJA)—somehow talked me into giving $1,200 to become a lifetime NAJA member when I was still a graduate student. It has been money well spent. I played a lot of pool with Patty Loew (Bad River Band of Lake Superior Ojibwe) and she continues to inspire me with her work as the director of the Center for Native American and Indigenous Research at Northwestern University.

Newswatch was a publication of the Center for Integration and Improvement of Journalism (CIIJ). It was updated with an educators' guide and then published as a magazine for many years. I was lucky enough to become its director after completing a PhD at the University of Michigan. While its director, I was elected President of NAJA and served in that role during the Unity 2008 Conference in Chicago. At that time, all of the Unity organization presidents were women.

I finished my college education at SF State after floundering at four community colleges (as well as another California State University); it took me seven years to get my Bachelor's degree. At SF State, I minored in American Indian Studies where I was lucky to have as my mentor Professor Elizabeth Parent who was the chair of that department, and the first Alaskan Native to receive a PhD. At that time, I did not even know what a PhD was. She encouraged me to continue my education and apply for the MA in ethnic studies at SF State. I was wait-listed for admission. When I got accepted to a doctoral program at the University of Michigan three years later, she told me that working toward a PhD was just paying penance for credentials. I still believe she was right; Betty is always right, and she is still my mentor.

I would not have completed my doctoral studies without Professor Travis Dixon (now at the University of Illinois-Urbana) who pushed me. He taught me to truly understand the impact that research could have on the wider society. As his research assistant for his groundbreaking work on representations of Black criminality in the news media, he allowed me to work with him at each step of the process so that I could understand and apply it in my future research. I thought of him frequently while writing this book, and how he called me his first "baby." While at Michigan I was lucky to meet Tara Young, who at the time was the president of Students of Color of Rackham. I couldn't have made it through this book without her support.

I am indebted to those who read drafts of this book. Dr. Victoria LaPoe (Citizen of the Cherokee Nation)—associate professor in the Scripps College of Communication at Ohio University—read the first draft of this manuscript. She provided much encouragement, and then became a terrific research partner for a number of other published journal articles including the first communication article to use Indigenous Standpoint Theory, which was published in 2021 in a special edition of the *Howard Journal of Communications* focused on the COVID pandemic and minority communities. Jim Wagstaffe (partner and co-founder of San Francisco-based law firm, WVBR LLP), read multiple drafts and helped me craft my underlying argument. Everyone needs a Jim Wagstaffe in their circle.

Professor Kristen Harrison (in Communication and Media at University of Michigan), and Professor Emeritus Rebecca Tallent (Cherokee) (in the School of Journalism and Mass Media at the University of Idaho) helped me navigate the racist and sexist world of peer-reviewed journal editors, and reminded me that it was not me who was the problem, it was the editors.

Dr. Ivana Markova helped me restart my research program after toiling as a department chair for six years. She re-taught me statistical analysis and made research fun again, even though we always spent most of our meetings not talking about research.

Nicolette Amstutz, my editor at Lexington Books, was wonderful and patient and encouraged me along the three-year-publishing journey.

This book would have been missing so much if it was not for the interviews and legal reviews of the book, so I express my deep appreciation to those who spent so much time on them. Thank you Patty Talahongva (Hopi), Bryan Pollard (citizen of Cherokee Nation), Deb Krol (Xolon Salinan), Paula Peters (Mashpee Wampanoag), Dan Lewerenz (Iowa Tribe of Kansas and Nebraska), Jim Kinsella (former editor of the *Cape Cod Times*), Greg Burton (executive editor of the *Arizona Republic*), Andrew Adams III (Muscogee Creek Nation), Allegra Collins (Black and Mvskoke), and other legal sources who chose to remain anonymous.

Arlinda Locklear deserves a special acknowledgment for her persistence in working for federal recognition for the Lumbee Tribe—and for not giving up hope after decades of effort. The Lumbee Tribe of North Carolina's journey toward federal recognition is another story that has been fraught with obstacles. Arlinda expects that recognition will occur in the future through legislation. She made the decision to become a lawyer as an adult when she was only twelve years old. An uncle who was just a teenager was arrested for a crime he did not commit. As Arlinda explained to me, "He was the only Native they could find on the street, and they put him in jail and beat the hell out of him to try to coerce a confession." The young Arlinda saw the pain it caused her grandfather and decided to go to law school to help stop the debasement of Indian people.

Without my uncle Kenny Adams' twenty-year fight for acknowledgment— our Tribe would not have received federal recognition. He inspired me to tell more stories to make federal recognition more than just a bunch of words. His interview provided the beautiful opening story about my grandmother Mary Alice Adams giving the first $20 toward the cost of federal recognition. That story changed how I wrote the book and it prompted me to want to use the photo of the turkey feather mantel made by my great grandmother Mollie Holmes Adams on the books cover. Her photo is below.

Pulitzer Prize winning photographer Kim Komenich took the photo of the porcupine quill medicine wheel made by Roberta Shields (Navajo and Cheyenne River Lakota Sioux). Kim is the most-humble award-winning photojournalist there is, and I'm honored to work with him at SF State. Simon Rogers, data editor at Google, graciously created the word clouds in chapter 7 to add a coolness factor.

Finally, I want to thank those closest to me for their unwavering support while writing this book: my partner Ed Lopez who never faulters; my son R. Armand Azocar who always makes me laugh; and my mom Nora Adams Azocar who keeps me on my toes.

This book was supported in part by the Dr. Paula M. Poindexter Research Grant from the Minorities and Communication Division of the Association for Education in Journalism and Mass Communication, and a mini-grant from SF State's College of Liberal and Creative Arts.

Chapter 1

Federal Recognition, Jim Crow, and the News Media

"It's an accident of history that there are so many non-federally recognized Tribes."[1] —Arlinda Locklear (Lumbee), the first Native woman to try a case before the Supreme Court

Native Americans are the only racial group often required to prove their identity to the non-Natives. The Tribes to which they belong often must substantiate their existence to the U.S. government prior to being given sovereign status. Native American Tribes that are not federally recognized spend decades gathering documentation to prove both that they are "Indians" and their continuing existence as self-governing communities. The Nations and Tribes that are the Indigenous people of the United States were autonomous Nations and Tribes prior to the European invasion that began with the first contact. They were self-governing and sovereign. But now, without federal acknowledgment, Tribes do not have the authority to make decisions on behalf of their members.

The fundamental problem is that Tribes without federal recognition cannot have a government-to-government relationship with the United States. Even Tribes that are part of the historical landscape of the United States (and commonly recognized as Tribes geographically, such as state-recognized Tribes) must solicit the U.S. government for the right of sovereignty. Legislation enacted to essentially eliminate Indigenous peoples and also the news media all too often make the process of acquiring federal recognition labor intensive and difficult.

Two laws symbolize tribal self-determination and self-governance. These are the Indian Self-Determination and Education Assistance Act of 1975 and the Tribal Self-Governance Act of 1994. These laws allowed tribal governments to provide services that otherwise would be provided by the United States. Furthermore, they upheld the principle of tribal consultation by requiring the federal government to consult with Tribes on federal actions, policies, rules, or regulations that directly affect them.[2]

However, the U.S. Congress gets to determine if Tribes possess the right of self-determination. A Tribe that is considered a "tribal entity" is referred to as a federally recognized Tribe. Tribes without this designation must seek federal recognition so that they may self-govern—or remain in limbo without self-determination rights. And that self-government is frequently at odds with those who want to control the economic resources that may come with self-governance.

Whether through past and current government policy, such as Jim Crow and/or eugenics laws enacted in the nineteenth and twentieth centuries, combined with centuries of inaccurate news media portrayals on which legislatures often rely for their information about "Indians," it is nearly impossible for some Tribes to prove that they are actually a "Tribe" in terms of federal recognition. Instead, it leaves tribal members of these (non-recognized) "groups" erased as though they never existed.

U.S. GOVERNMENT CONGRESSIONAL ACTS

Indian policy in the nineteenth century was enacted with the purpose of either separation from, or annihilation or assimilation of, Tribes and their members—a way of erasure of large numbers of peoples. The U.S. government from 1872 to 1874 permitted white traders to slaughter buffalo in order to rid the geographic area termed the "Plains" Tribes, such as the Cheyenne, Kiowa, and Comanche.[3,4] The Dawes Act and other statutes broke up tribal communal lands into individual Indian allotments; consequently, those allotted lands could be sold to whites or seized for nonpayment of taxes.[5]

Although not as overt, current federal policies also advance annihilation and assimilation. For example, the U.S. Census Bureau provides definitions of racial groups based on origin. It defines a "White" person as one "having origins in any of the original peoples of Europe, the Middle East, or North Africa." It defines a "Black" (or "African American") person as a "person having origins in any of the Black racial groups of Africa." On the other hand—for Indians—there is added language requiring ties to a Tribe. "American Indian or Alaska Native" is "a person having origins in any of the original peoples of North and South America (including Central America) and who maintains tribal affiliation or community attachment."[6] Thus, the government can decide who is Indian (and what constitutes a Tribe), so it can prevent Indians from being Indian, as well as a Tribe from being a Tribe.

WHITE SUPREMACY—RELATIONSHIP TO THE EMBRACEMENT OF JIM CROW AND EUGENICS

The legendary Native woman Matoaka, more commonly known now as Pocahontas, was a member of the Pamunkey Tribe of what subsequently became the state of Virginia. Ironically—given the historical idea of Native people that she represents—Pocahontas would not have been considered part of an Indian Nation as defined by the federal government until the twenty-first century.

In July 2015, the Pamunkey Tribe finally received federal recognition (acknowledging that the Tribe was—indeed—a tribal entity). This was a moment of triumph for the Pamunkey, as well as the six other state-recognized Tribes in Virginia: the Chickahominy, the Eastern Chickahominy, the Rappahannock, the Monacan, the Nansemond, and the Upper Mattaponi, which the author is a citizen of. The Pamunkey Tribe began its pursuit of federal recognition in the 1970s through the Bureau of Indian Affairs process of federal acknowledgment. Due to the vicious cycle within which the Pamunkey Tribe found itself entangled, the Tribe eventually resorted to seeking recognition through the legislative process. (All of these processes are described in detail later in this book.) That entanglement was due in large measure to laws enacted to rid the state of Virginia of its Indian population in the early part of the 1900s; this made it nearly impossible for the Pamunkey Tribe to prove it was a Tribe. Consequently, the Pamunkey sought recognition through an Act of Congress with the other state-recognized Tribes of Virginia but then decided to go back to the BIA process separate from the coalition of Tribes. This was due to the reality that—unlike all but one of the other Tribes in Virginia, the Mattaponi[7]—it has a reservation.

In 1924, Virginia's Racial Integrity Act institutionalized the "one-drop rule." This rule was that any person with even one ancestor tracing to Sub-Saharan Africa was considered to be "Negro"; it was this Act that outlawed interracial marriage. The Act was spearheaded by Walter Ashby Plecker, who was a physician, eugenicist, and avowed white supremacist; he was also the registrar from 1912 to 1946 of Virginia's Bureau of Vital Statistics. Plecker directed other Registrars in Virginia to delete "Indian" on birth certificates and write in "colored."

In 1943, Plecker wrote a letter addressed to "Local registrars, clerks, legislators, and others responsible for, and interested in, the prevention of racial intermixture." He described in this letter how the Act had worked to exterminate all Indians in Virginia as embodied in the following sentence: "Public records in the office of the Bureau of Vital Statistics, and in the State Library, indicate that there does not exist today a descendant of the Virginia ancestors claiming to be an Indian who is unmixed with negro blood."[8]

Virginia's Tribes continued to struggle to receive federal recognition because they could not prove their continuity of heritage through the historic documentation that federal administrative acknowledgment requires, and a major reason was the reclassification of Native peoples through the Racial Integrity Act.[9] Problematically for Virginia's tribal peoples, this Act essentially erased the entire Native American population of Virginia with a pen—that can be viewed as a "paper genocide" in its impact on them.

Paper genocide is the deliberate and systematic destruction of a culture, language, and identity as a unique racial group by way of the illegal and oppressive reclassification imposed on racial groups through government records.[10] It was not until 1967 that the "one-drop rule" was overturned by the U.S. Supreme Court.[11] However, reversing one's status back to Indian was prevented because Native people born before 1967 and not living on a government-regulated Indian reservation, or in a community with a significant Native population ("Native lands") were still listed as "colored" by vital records offices. In 1997, the Monacan Tribe requested legislation be enacted to correct the legacy of the unfair racial integrity law and, thereby, provide an avenue for individual tribal members to correct racial designations without having to pay an administrative fee.[12]

The issue of a tribe's "rights" is significant in a time when even federally recognized Tribes are facing challenges to their sovereign rights, if such "rights" conflict with the status quo historically favoring white economic elites. In 2018, the Dakota Access Pipeline (DAPL) public protests, known as No DAPL or #NoDAPL,[13] were prompted by the Standing Rock Sioux Tribe, a sovereign Nation at odds with the powerful fossil fuel industry. Due to its wealth and political power, the fossil fuel industry is a significant commercial contributor to curtailing sovereign tribal rights.[14,15]

Unlike much of what happens in Indian Country, the aforementioned No DAPL protests made international headlines. This was largely due to the publicity about the protests reported via social media, as well as independent news organizations such as Democracy Now![16] Indian Country is typically not included in news media coverage except—as in the case of the No DAPL protests—when tribal members are seen as a disruption to the interests of white economic elites, in times of civil strife, and when tribally controlled gaming operations threaten the economic interests of corporations and other typical economic elites in the United States. In such times, the news media become an important arbiter of Native rights and entitlements. Indigenous media, however, play an important role in mobilizing Native communities by providing accurate and critical thinking in their coverage to their citizens.[17]

Although the news media and their historical influence on politics have been well documented, little research exists on news media coverage of any of the Tribes which are seeking federal recognition.

The questions which need more attention on the part of the field of journalism include the following: Does the news media cover Tribes that are seeking recognition? What are the predominant frames (or perspectives) found in that coverage? Does the news media consider sovereignty in the coverage of "Indians?" Can the customary news media practice of agenda setting and framing regarding the role of the hegemony provide an insight into the level of racism in reporting in the mainstream media? Do decolonizing theories provide a more complete perspective about media coverage? What role does tribal involvement in the gaming industry play in news coverage pertaining to a Tribe? How does news coverage of issues related to federal recognition differ between mainstream and Indigenous publications/media?

These are some of the questions this book seeks to address, and thereby examine how institutional and structural racism specifically impact media coverage of issues relevant to Indigenous individuals and Tribes. In illustration of the impact of institutional and structural racism as embedded in news media, this book includes an examination of the predominant frames utilized in the recent acknowledgment cases of Virginia Indian Tribes. Specifically, the case studies in this book consider whether the news media embraced the "gaming" frame more than the "sovereignty" frame since gaming became a viable economic industry in Indian County, particularly in 2015 when the Pamunkey Tribe received federal recognition through the BIA's federal acknowledgment process, and in 2018 when six additional Virginia Tribes were acknowledged through the legislative process.

THE ROLE OF THE NEWS MEDIA: ANALYTIC FRAMEWORKS

The news media's role in perpetuating ignorance and stereotypes about the sovereignty of Native Nations is examined and revealed in this book through investigating how news media practices of agenda setting and framing influence the coverage (and, therefore, public perspectives) of federal recognition. It also examines how hegemony works in the decision-making process behind agenda setting and federal recognition. Furthermore, it analyzes mainstream news media coverage from the perspective of Western theories of communication to Indigenous news coverage using Indigenous Standpoint Theory as part of the ongoing academic efforts to decolonize research. An overview of these theories is provided below prior to considering the intersection of these theories with coverage of Indian County in the mainstream media versus U.S. Indigenous media.

Framing

Framing is an important concept in thinking about how journalists report and present news stories. In other words, framing essentially provides the parameters around how a situation (i.e., a news story) can influence how people think about the situation presented; therefore, framing may have a political impact on the news media consumer.[18] In terms of framing, this book considers how the greater prevalence of news articles referring to tribal-controlled "gaming" and framing the stories through frequent use of terms such as "casino" and "gambling" as opposed to other tribal-related stories may influence public perception of federal recognition for Native Tribes. In this book, it is theorized that these frames may perpetuate the notion that Tribes only seek federal recognition in order to open a casino, rather than primarily for self-determination of the Tribe.

Agenda Setting

The agenda-setting theory argues that the news media sets the public agenda. According to this theory, while the news media may not exactly tell people what to think, they tell people what to think about. As aptly stated in an article in 1972 in *Public Opinion Quarterly*, "In choosing and displaying news, editors, newsroom staff and broadcasters play an important part in shaping political reality. Readers learn not only about a given issue, but also how much importance to attach to that issue from the amount of information in a news story and its position."[19] In terms of mainstream news media coverage, "stories" about Indigenous Nations are generally scarce,[20] and—when news coverage does occur about Tribes seeking federal recognition—their desire for self-determination is trivialized through a news media emphasis on casino control as the dominant issue.

Hegemony is the term used to describe how a population's leaders and the leadership structure exert control over its citizens through governmental or social means[21] In the United States, white privilege is maintained through hegemony as engendered in institutionalized and structural racism. The mainstream media can be complicit in this white "privileging" over non-whites in the United States by reproducing and reinforcing ideas that promote the status quo while de-emphasizing ideas that enable increased attention on issues that would promote increased power on the part of non-white U.S. residents.[22] For Tribes, this translates to news coverage reinforcing the corporate dominance and overall white "power" to solely maintain ownership of the Nation's financial and wealth-building resources, inclusive of the gaming industry, and irrespective of a tribe's rights of self-determination and/or legal rights to decide whether or not to consider a gaming operation.

Both of these above-described theories are constructed by Western academic traditions, rather than Indigenous traditions. To understand the Indigenous perspective on how this coverage affects communities, this research also applies Indigenous Standpoint theory as described below.

INDIGENOUS STANDPOINT THEORY

Indigenous Standpoint theory contextualizes content within meaningful cultural and social perspectives to Indigenous individuals and groups.[23,24] It emphasizes the research findings of Indigenous scholars because of their ability to understand the complexities of Indigenous communities and how structural racism pervades and impacts their issues and choices.[25] Unlike the two previously described Western academic theories, this theory provides a framework for Native American academics to define research, methodologies, and the interpretation of results in a culturally appropriate way because of their "lived" reality within a racist society.[26] In contrast to Western theories, this theory acknowledges the family collective consciousness, politics, and history of Indigenous peoples.[27]

LINKING RESEARCH METHODOLOGIES AND THEORETICAL BASES TO NEWS MEDIA

Tribes continue to strive for federal recognition, and the news media continue to exert their influence on public opinion and public policy affecting Tribes and their citizens. By examining how past coverage has prioritized gaming (e.g., casinos) over sovereignty in news coverage, reporters, editors, and producers of news media can better understand how they perpetuate inaccuracies and stereotypes about Indigenous people. Additionally—by understanding decolonizing methodologies—researchers within the journalism field can aid in the reframing of news reporting. In this way, a shift in news reporting can occur that reveals the importance of federal recognition to both the Tribes that are seeking it and the public at large. Utilizing research methodologies that reverse the bias inherent in Western academic theories that perpetuate delegitimization of the experiences and issues of all non-white populations allows the true story of the struggle for federal recognition as experienced by Native peoples to be told and understood.

COVERAGE OF FEDERAL RECOGNITION

Although legal, anthropological, archeological, environmental, and cultural studies have been published about the federal recognition process, there is a dearth of research related to this topic in the fields of communication and journalism. In fact, no articles about federal recognition and Tribes exist in the Communication and Mass Media Complete Database.[28] Of the seventy-eight articles listed in Academic Search Complete, only thirty-four are peer reviewed;[29] three articles (from law journals) examine tribally owned/operated gambling facilities or casinos. A vital reason that this academic research be conducted within the fields of communication and journalism is that it provides the theoretical basis by which current and future generations of journalists should be trained. For journalism to begin a change from the status quo to accurately cover Indigenous people and Tribes, it is crucial for anyone in the field of journalism to grasp how institutional and structural racism, inclusive of governmental policies and laws, influences mainstream media to control public perceptions of the following: (1) who has the right to be Indian, (2) what gives Indians the right to have a sovereign relationship with the U.S. government, and (3) how those rights are threatened when Native peoples exert their sovereign status to develop wealth-generating gaming operations.

Chapter 2 of this book describes how the U.S. government (all three branches) has been instrumental in deciding who is Indian and how this designation does not generally correspond with how Indigenous Nations actually define their "members."

Chapter 3 is an examination of the role of institutionalized and systemic racism in the federal recognition process; it shows how white supremacy (embodied in racist laws and policies) have thwarted the process of attaining federal recognition by Tribes.

Chapter 4 is focused on how framing theory, agenda-setting theory, and hegemonic theories enable inaccurate and stereotypical news media portrayals of Native people that perpetuate and uphold white privilege and the oppression of people Indigenous people.

Chapter 5 explains how Indigenous Standpoint Theory can be used to counteract the harmful consequences of Native American-focused research that is grounded in a racist perspective.

Chapter 6 examines the history of news media coverage of federal recognition from the vantage point of published research on federal recognition in the field of communications including a discussion of how the news coverage contributed to gaming becoming the biggest news story in Indian Country.

Chapter 7 describes the results of a news content analysis over a forty-year period pertaining to federal recognition. Inclusive of describing a content analysis performed on more than 3,500 news stories, this chapter reveals how news stories conflated federal recognition with gaming for more than four decades.

Chapter 8 examines the coverage of the federal recognition of the seven Tribes in Virginia. While one case study is focused on the Pamunkey Tribe's experience, the other is focused on the six Tribes that received recognition through legislation on January 28, 2018: the Chickahominy, the Eastern Chickahominy, the Upper Mattaponi, the Rappahannock, the Monacan, and the Nansemond.

Chapter 9 compares Indigenous news coverage of federal recognition during the same period as the news coverage by mainstream news media. Although there are not as many published articles overall in Indigenous news media as in non-Indigenous news media regarding federal recognition, this is primarily to the reality that most Indigenous print news media are not daily publications and may have fewer staff journalists. However, Indigenous publications published a far greater number of articles on federal recognition as compared to non-Indigenous publications in proportion to their small size.

In chapter 10, interviews conducted with Indigenous journalists and Indigenous legal experts are utilized to aid in understanding what federal recognition actually means for Tribes, and how the coverage of recognition can boost empowerment efforts of Indigenous and other marginalized communities, political leaders, and journalists. Likewise, this chapter also shows how Indigenous Standpoint Theory plays a role in Indigenous news media publications.

One of the most prevalent current stereotypes about Native peoples and Native Nations is that all are involved with casinos and encourage gambling. Gaming operations are complicated and take time to build, and federal recognition is not about casinos: it is about our identity and self-determination. Therefore, chapter 11 describes the process of opening a gaming operation and explains how federal recognition does not equate to involvement in the gaming industry.

This book concludes in chapter 12 with an action plan to promote future news media coverage of federal recognition for Tribes from an Indigenous standpoint rather than a vantage point of white privilege.

American Indian? Native American? Indian? Native? Indigenous? These are all terms used to describe the Indigenous people of North and South America. Sometimes one term seems more applicable when used in a nonfiction book focused on the experiences of Indigenous peoples than another.

Although many Native academics use the term Native American, this book uses the term Indigenous as it is more accurate than incorporating the term "America"—since Indigenous people were inhabiting this continent long before it became "America." It also frequently uses "Native" for the same reason. The term seems to fit the descriptions in this book so that the lived experience of the people and Tribes described is evoked for the readers. Since that lived experience is not static, an attempt is made to demonstrate changed realities through fluidity in word choice. "Tribe" always appears in its formal, capitalized form to respect the nations the term represents, just as other nations are capitalized.

Meanwhile, "Indian Country" is a legal term used in Title 18 of the U.S. Code.[30] Whenever possible in this book, the actual name of the Tribe or Nation is used rather than an all-encompassing term such as Indigenous. After all, Indigenous people are diverse—even if the unique diversity has been effectively erased in most news stories about them presented by the non-Indigenous news media.

NOTES

1. Arlinda Locklear interview.
2. U.S. Department of the Interior, Bureau of Indian Affairs (BIA). "Frequently Asked Questions." www.bia.gov/frequently-asked-questions
3. Rister, 1929.
4. Matthiessen, 1959.
5. Pevar, 2004.
6. U.S. Census Bureau. About the Topic of Race. www.census.gov/topics/population/race/about.html.
7. The Mattaponi Tribe is a separate Tribe from the Mattaponi
8. Murray, 1987.
9. Moten, 1999.
10. Paper genocide is not broadly embraced as a term in the academic literature but is embraced in this book per its usage in: The Daily Kos, How Jim Crow Practiced Paper Genocide Against Native American Indians, https://www.dailykos.com/stories/2016/6/25/1542478/-How-Jim-Crow-Practiced-Paper-Genocide-Against-Native-American-Indians? Accessed March 18, 2019 and on the website Paper Genocide http://www.papergenocide.org/.
11. *Loving v. Virginia*, 388 U.S. 1 (1967).
12. Cook, 2002.
13. The archive can be found at https://www.nodaplarchive.com/.
14. This includes a current attempt to overturn the seemingly unrelated Indian Child Welfare Act. Nagle, 2021.
15. In December 2016, Hilary C. Tompkins, the solicitor of the Department of the Interior (DOI), issued a memorandum titled Tribal Treaty and Environmental

Statutory Implications of the Dakota Access Pipeline. In this memorandum, Solicitor Tompkins stated—while the environmental assessment of the U.S. *Army Corps of Engineers* (ACE) acknowledged the Standing Rock Sioux's concerns regarding the DAPL pipeline—the DOI determined the pipeline would not affect the Tribe's reservation or residents as this ACE assessment "fails to consider the government-to-government relationship with the Tribe and other issues raised above concerning the various environmental statutes applicable to this project." Moreover, Tompkins concluded, "there is ample legal justification for the Corps to exercise its discretion to suspend or revoke the existing Section 408 permit and/or postpone a decision on the proposed easement conditional on additional analysis and government-to-government consultation concerning the tribal-specific issues."

Furthermore, The Solicitor specifies that if the ACE authorized the easement, additional tribal consultation would be needed to protect the Standing Rock Sioux Tribe's rights and interests. The Barack Obama Administration denied the pipeline permit, but President Donald J. Trump overturned it on February 27, 2017. Therefore, the pipeline became operational on June 1, 2017 (Cama, 2017). Meanwhile, five oil spills occurred in the first six months of the pipeline's operation (Brown, 2018).

16. Moore & Lanthorn, 2017.
17. LaPoe et al., 2018.
18. Entman, 1993.
19. McCombs & Shaw, 1972.
20. Monet, 2019.
21. Hall, 1977.
22. Heider, 2000.
23. Rigne, 1999.
24. Foley, 2003.
25. Rigney, 1999.
26. Rigney, 1997.
27. Nakata, 2007.
28. Accessed May 30, 2019.
29. Search terms were "federal recognition" or "federal Acknowledgment" and American Indian or Native American or Tribe or Nation. Accessed April 23, 2018.
30. 18 U.S. Code § 1151 Indian Country Defined.

Chapter 2

Who Is Indian and Who Decides?

The U.S. government has been instrumental in deciding who is Indian. However, this designation doesn't necessarily correspond with how Tribes define their members (as discussed later in this book). Due in large part to the United States with the mass media in which Native people are presented stereotypically, "Indians"—even at the current time—all too often feel that they must look and act like "real Indians" to be considered "authentic."[1]

Not only can this be damaging to the self-esteem, this non-Native determination of who is Indian relegates Native people to a static past rather than in a dynamic context.[2] For most non-Indigenous people in the United States, "true" Indians are viewed as those living only on reservations and in poverty and who wear braids in their hair and feathers on their clothing. The inherent problem is this has an adverse impact on Native peoples and their communities (as it would for anyone disallowed such self-determination/self-identification).

Indigenous peoples have been social constructions since their first recorded encounters with Europeans. Christopher Columbus coined the term "los Indios" when he thought he had landed on an island off Asia. In Columbus' time, "India" was the term used for all of Asia located east of the Indus River (which is the derivation of "Indies" as a word[3,4,5]) and was the most comprehensive description for all of the area he claimed under royal patent.[6,7] The inaccurate term of "Indians" (with all of its demeaning connotations) was embedded in children's minds in the United States mainly through the education system.

As stated in Dunbar-Ortiz and Gilio-Whitaker's 2016 book on pervasive myths in the United States about Native Americans, "The image of the savage, innocent, nature-loving being is the one still expected today by the majority of people, American and abroad, as that is the image seen by young children and throughout mass media."[8] Contemporary Native people (especially those who do not live on reservations) are not usually considered in U.S. society as authentic "Indians" even though nearly 80 percent of Native people do not live on reservations or other lands designated as trust lands[9] and more than half of that 80 percent live in urban areas.[10]

In theory, Tribes have the right to determine their membership—whether through ancestral lineage, blood quantum (cultural identity based on the fraction of blood ascribed to a tribal member), or historical roles of an individual, whether they have ancestral lineage or not.[11] However—in practice—Indigenous people have only rarely been allowed to define themselves by their own cultural norms and practices, nor have they been afforded the agency to define their relationships to the United States.[12]

As the "colonizers," powerful white people in leadership positions have been the "classifiers" and Natives and other non-white residents of the United States the "classified." Yet, this racism toward Natives has included classification utilizing "content of specific imagery and the context of a particular history and space."[13] Problematically for Native peoples, that history and space has remained static since the colonizers first arrived on the continent.

Native people belong to a distinct racial group, and to a distinct legal group. However, no one method exists to define who gets to be Indian, and multiple definitions exist. For example, *Halbert v. U.S.* 1931—focused on the power to determine Native identity for the purposes of legal rights, policies, and programs.[14] And, *Simmons v. Eagle Seelatsee* decided that Congress can determine who is Native for federal purposes: Congress and its agents have the power to define which persons "should be treated and regarded as members of an Indian Tribe and entitled to enrollment therein."[15] So, a person can identify as Indian (as the plaintiffs in this case did) but still fail to qualify for enrollment based on congressional standards.

Although Tribes have the power to determine who is a member for tribal purposes, they do not have that same authority for state and/or federal purposes.[16] According to the 1982 amended regulations of the Indian Reorganization Act ([IRA], 1934[17]), an Indian is defined as the following: a member of a federally recognized Tribe, descendants of members of recognized tribes that were residing on an Indian reservation on June 1, 1934, or a person who has one half or more Indian blood.

Therefore, even if an individual Tribe and the U.S. government use the same method to determine a person's "Indian-ness," such as through a combination of blood quantum and ancestry, the outcomes may not necessarily be the same for an individual person. One commonly used method relies on the 120-year-old Dawes Act; another method relies on the nebulous notion of blood quantum. Moreover, a particular Tribe may base enrollment on a different level of blood quantum than another Tribe. While Tribes are not required to use blood quantum as a method, the federal government has wielded its authority in this area; this has resulted in most federally recognized Tribes requiring a specific level of blood quantum in order to qualify for tribal citizenship.[18]

Discussed below are both the Dawes Act and concept of blood quantum to show how each—intentionally—have served to decrease the "count" of the Indigenous population, with resultant erasure as "Indians," succeeded in further confusing the perceptions of Indian identity.

THE DAWES ACT

Under the guise of a compromise with westward expansion and protecting Native property rights, the U.S. congress in 1887 passed the General Allotment Act (or Dawes Act) which was named after its author, Massachusetts Senator Henry Dawes, "friend" of the Indian. This legislation allowed for the U.S. President to seize commonly held reservation land, as well as break it up and create individual allotments of that land. Surplus land was sold to non-Indian settlers. Meanwhile, Indians had to register on a tribal "roll" to be granted allotments. Once enrolled on a tribal "roll," the Native person's name was placed on the "Dawes rolls." Through this process, the BIA and the Secretary of the Interior used the roll to determine the eligibility of individual Indians for land distribution.

Senator Dawes' belief (as embodied in the Dawes Act) was that if Natives owned land, they would assimilate more quickly. Under the Dawes Act, the allotments (160 acres of farmland or 320 acres of grazing land) were distributed essentially as such: to each head of a family, one-quarter of a section; to each single person over eighteen years of age, one-eighth of a section; to each orphan child under eighteen years of age, one-eighth of a section; and to each other single person under eighteen years now living, or who may be born prior to the date of the order of the president directing an allotment of the lands embraced in any reservation, one-sixteenth of a section.[19]

More than 250,000 Native people applied to the commission for enrollment to receive land; only around 100,000 were approved. Indigenous landholdings were reduced from 138 million acres in 1887 to merely 48 million in 1934. Furthermore, nearly 20 million acres (of the total 48 million acres) were desert or semiarid, so not suitable for farming,[20] and land patents could be issued only after being held in trust for twenty-five years by the Secretary of the Interior. Land could not be sold, nor could the title be transferred during the time held in trust; once the patent was issued, the owner became subject to the laws of the state or territory of the allocated land.

Consequently, the allotments only succeeded in propelling more Native people into poverty since few had the capital to buy the equipment needed to run farms, even when the land was not utterly unsuitable for farming. When real-estate taxes came due, they were forced to sell their allotments or they lost their land to debt-induced foreclosures.

Although children, who usually had been sent away to boarding schools, could inherit allotments, they could not care for their allotments (e.g., cultivate crops) but because they were legally confined to these boarding schools. Native persons with multiple children also were ensnared in the ambiguity of ownership, because—when several heirs inherited an allotment—the size of the holding received by each heir was often too small for any income generation from farming that holding.[21]

Appointed by President Franklin D. Roosevelt, Indian Commissioner John Collier wrote in a letter signed by Lynn Frazier, chairman of the Senate Indian Investigating Subcommittee, the following regarding the practice of selling allotments on the death of the original allottee:[22]

> The consequences are mathematically certain . . . the allotted Indians of the second generation largely become landless. By the time the third generation has arrived, substantially all of the allotted Indian land will have passed into white ownership.

Only 36,000 acres of the land originally allocated under the Dawes Act remained under Native control by the year 2000.[23] Currently, the Cherokee, Creek, Choctaw, Chickasaw, and Seminole Tribes still use the Dawes rolls to determine membership, although they were allowed to be exempt from it following the passage of the Curtis Act in 1898.[24] In 1893, President Grover Cleveland created and appointed members to the Dawes Commission. This commission was tasked to negotiate to acquire a solution with these five Tribes and—as a result—several federal laws (including the Curtis Act) were passed that allotted a share of common property to members of these Tribes. However, the share of common property was contingent on abolishing their tribal governments and recognizing state and federal laws.[25]

The Dawes Act departed from earlier Indian policies regarding removal, treaties, and reservations. However—in its willful ignorance of Native culture—it presumed that assimilation would be "better" for Native people. Intrinsic laws such as the Dawes Act was the goal of decimating the population of Indians.

BLOOD QUANTUM

Indian blood quantum was a concept derived to further reduce the number of Native people in the United States.[26] The use of blood quantum most likely originated in 1705 when the colony of Virginia implemented a series of laws that specifically denied human rights to persons deemed to be negroes, mulattos, and/or Indians. In instances when a person did not clearly appear to match solely one of the categories (negroes, mulattos, or Indians), "the child of an Indian, and the child, grandchild or great grandchild of a negro shall be deemed accounted, held and taken to be a mulatto."[27]

Virginia may also have been the first to define—in 1785—a specific amount of blood in defining a person as mulatto[28] (which was utilized for various purposes) per the following passage:

> [E]very person other than a negro, of whose grandfathers or grandmothers any one is or shall have been a negro, although all his other progenitors, except that descending from the negro shall have been white persons . . . and so every person who shall have one fourth or more negro blood, shall in like manner be deemed a mulatto.[29]

The 1934 Indian Reorganization Act marked the beginning of the widespread use of blood quantum; it established procedures for Tribes to adopt constitutions to define their membership. This created major ambiguity in determining tribal membership.

Blood quantum was originally determined by ancestry and appearance. As generations intermarried and produced offspring, that "quantum of blood" in a given person decreased. Basically, the offspring of parents with different tribal affiliations were not considered "full-bloods" of either Tribe. In fact, they were considered to have half or less blood—depending on the status of the parents of either Tribe, further reducing the population of both Tribes and the individuals in those Tribes.

Because Indians with a drop of "Negro blood" were considered Colored, Tribes faced pressures to intermarry only with whites or solely to marry each other. Tribes deemed to have too much Negro blood were in danger of being subjected to Jim Crow laws.

For example, in 1857, a group of white locals took guns from Pamunkey tribal members in Virginia. When the Tribe complained to the governor, he agreed that the law did not apply to Indians, but that "if any become one fourth mixed with the negro race then they may be treated as free negroes or mulattoes."[30] This had major consequences for already vulnerable Tribes.

In 1886, tribal law prohibited Pamunkeys from intermarrying with blacks, as stated in the following: "No member of the Pamunkey Indian Tribe shall intermarry with any [sic] Nation except White or Indian under penalty of forfeiting their rights in Town."[31] Jack Forbes' speculative account of what those in an "Indian-Black marriage" might be subject to illustrates the complexity of this particular form of racial oppression:[32]

. . . in Virginia, a Pamunkey family might well have been viciously shattered in this [20th] century by the state law which allows "Indians" living on the Pamunkey Reservation to have up to 1/32 African ancestry and still be "Indian." But if they moved to Richmond or just across the reservation boundary, they would become "colored" if they had any African blood whatsoever. Moreover, those who had more than 1/32nd African blood could not remain on the reservation as "Indians," even though they might have lived there all of their lives.[33]

Ironically—in their petition for federal recognition 130 years later—the Pamunkey Tribe would be accused of racism against African Americans based on forced acquiescence to this law. The Pamunkey Tribe conceded to Jim Crow laws to maintain being Pamunkey, but then those laws were used against them. It is the pernicious nature of white hegemony that it has the power to pit racial groups without such power against each other, and thereby further reduce the power and self-determination capacity of both vulnerable groups.

NOTES

1. Dunbar-Ortiz & Gilio-Whitaker, 2016.
2. Berkhofer, Jr., 1978.
3. Berkhofer, Jr., 1978.
4. Lach, 1965.
5. Morison, 1974.
6. Berkhofer, Jr. 1978.
7. Dippie, 1982.
8. Dunbar-Ortiz & Gilio-Whitaker, 2016.
9. The U.S. government holds the title to most tribal land for the benefit of existing and future tribal citizens. Trust land is subject to tribal government authority and not to state law, which gives Tribes the ability to form their own governments and to develop and enforce laws. But land use requires the approval of federal government.
10. Norris, Vines, & Hoeffel, 2012.
11. Schmidt, 2011.
12. Gonzales, 1998.
13. Berkhofer, Jr., 1978.
14. U.S. Supreme Court. *Halbert v. U.S.*, 283 U.S. 753 [1931]
15. U.S. Supreme Court. *Simmons v. Eagle Seelatsee*, 244 F. Supp. 808, 813-15 (E. D. Wash. 1965), *aff'd per curiam*, 384 U.S. 209 1966.
16. Pevar, 2004.
17. The 1934 act does not take nonfederally recognized Tribes into account but only applies to federally recognized Tribes.
18. TallBear, 2004.

19. Transcript of *Dawes Act* (See: www.ourdocuments.gov/doc.php?flash=true&doc=50)
20. Collier, 1934.
21. Dawes Act, 1887.
22. Phillip, 1977.
23. Pevar, 2004.
24. Section 8 of the Curtis Act (U.S., Statutes at Large 39:495, 1898) specified groups that were to be exempt from the law. It stated that "the provisions of this act shall not extend to the territory occupied by the Cherokees, Creeks, Choctaws, Chickasaws, Seminoles, and Osage, Miamies and Peorias, and Sacs and Foxes, in the Indian Territory, nor to any of the reservations of the Seneca Nation of New York Indians in the State of New York, nor to that strip of territory in the State of Nebraska adjoining the Sioux Nation on the south."
25. For an excellent description on how allotment laws were used to reduce Indian lands even further, listen to "This Land" a podcast by journalist Rebecca Nagle.
26. Jaimes, 1992.
27. Forbes, 2000.
28. Spruhan, 2006.
29. State Law of Virginia. Slaves, Free Negroes and Mulattoes, Va. Acts § 5.11 [1785].
30. Roundtree, 1976.
31. Adams, 2016.
32. Recommended for a comprehensive examination of the relationships between African Americans and Native Americans and the legal foundations of racialized thinking is the following book: Coleman, 2013.
33. Forbes, 1990.

Chapter 3

Federal Recognition and White Supremacy

Tribes that hope to petition for federal recognition face an uphill battle of bureaucracy meant to ensure their eventual demise and become entangled in it. Federal policies and laws have slowly chipped away at tribal rights—making it even more difficult for tribal entities to prove that they are a Tribe, and to prove that their members are "Indians." This is how the erasure of Indigenous people continues to persist in the United States, despite a broader public recognition of the historical disempowerment of people of color due to the structural racism perpetrated upon them for centuries.

INDIAN REORGANIZATION ACT

Also known as the Wheeler–Howard Act, the Indian Reorganization Act (IRA) of 1934[1] was designed to "rehabilitate the Indian's economic life and to give him a chance to develop the initiative destroyed by a century of oppression and paternalism." The IRA allowed Indigenous communities residing on reservations to create tribal governments and helped these governments defend their rights and "press local and federal officials to reverse the century-long decline in tribal sovereignty." The IRA sought to restore tribal governments, prohibited further allotment of tribal land, and authorized the Secretary of the Interior to add lands to existing reservations, to create reservations for Tribes that had lost their land, and to restore land declared surplus under the Dawes Act [aka General Allotment Act] of 1887.[2] It also persuaded Tribes to adopt constitutions, create federally chartered corporations, and assert their powers of self-government.

The IRA abolished the allotments of the Dawes Act, provided a framework for reservation communities to set up tribal governments, and helped these newly formed governments assert their rights and compel government officials to overturn the century-long decline in tribal sovereignty. Although the IRA increased Indigenous landholdings by more than 2 million acres and provided funding for infrastructure on reservations, it has been rightly criticized as paternalistic since Tribes were not consulted in its development and were still subject to federal control. The IRA also suggested Anglo-European systems of government for Tribes, and colonial ideals of "Indianness," by designating how Tribes could define their own membership.

During the congressional hearings in which debate over the IRA occurred, a disagreement arose concerning who was to be defined as an Indian. Congress resolved this area of disagreement by defining "Indian" to include three classes of people, and each determined by blood quantum, or degree of blood, as described earlier in this chapter. This legally restricted "Indian" to mean:

1. All persons of Indian descent who are members of a recognized Tribe, whether or not residing on an Indian reservation and regardless of the degree of blood.
2. All persons who are descendants of any such members of recognized tribes residing within an Indian reservation on June 1, 1934, regardless of blood.
3. Persons of one-half or more Indian blood, whether or not affiliated with a recognized Tribe and whether or not they have ever resided on an Indian reservation.

Many Tribes adopted the practice of using blood quantum for membership, and some Tribes continue to use blood quantum to define themselves and their numbers, although not generally based solely on it. Some Tribes use cultural, economic, residency, and history for determinations,[3] and other Tribes require their members to have a minimum of tribal blood to be enrolled in the Tribe (e.g., one-half degree, one-quarter degree, or one-eighth degree) of blood quantum. Given the high level of intermarrying that occurs among citizens of different Tribes, if the practice continues to use blood quantum over other cultural norms, Native people may soon cease to "exist" and erasure will have been achieved.

TERMINATION

In 1953, Congress approved House Resolution 108. This terminated the federal government's sovereign relationship with five of the largest American Indian Tribes.[4] In 1960, as Cold War ideologies took hold, Indians were often viewed as aliens. And during this period, land owned by Tribes was considered Communist, and, therefore, un-American.[5]

The federal policy from the mid-1940s through mid-1960s of termination[6] commenced the end of the government-to-government relationship between some Tribes and the U.S. termination disbanded the governments of what had formerly been federally recognized Tribes, removed their tax exemptions, ended federal assistance to them, and extinguished some Tribes' hunting and fishing rights.[7] It also discontinued federal obligations to these Tribes, dismantled reservation land bases, and decentralized the administration of Indian affairs. Additionally, it relocated or resulted in the relocation of some Native people to urban areas.[8]

Utah Senator Arthur Watkins and BIA Commissioner Dillon Myers billed termination as an Indian freedom program. Its pretext was that Tribes would be emancipated from paternalism and, thus, the discriminatory practices and policies that negatively affected them would be lifted. It was promoted under the guise of creating formal equality, facilitating self-reliance by speeding up assimilation efforts, and bestowing Indians with citizenship. Instead, it caused economic, political, and psychological hardships to Tribes that were terminated, as well as to tribal members who were relocated to urban areas.[9] It succeeded in tearing families and communities apart.

In the six decades since the termination policy began, Tribes have slowly become recognized as sovereign nations within the United States; some of them now can determine their own future paths. However, the structural barriers of racism, resultant from white supremacy, still impede Native peoples to be acknowledged as federally recognized Tribes, so the destructiveness of termination as the federal policy remains.

Importance of Federal Recognition

As stated by Lumbee attorney Arlinda Locklear, who has worked decades to help Tribes with their petitions, recognition is important because it allows Tribes to control their own destiny.[10] It is important to realize that—prior to the 1870s—the recognition of a Tribe by the U.S. government was a simple acknowledgment that a Tribe existed.

By negotiating treaties or enacting laws regarding the Tribes, the U.S. government informally acknowledged a Tribe existed as a formal entity. However, "acknowledgement" began to be implemented more formally in the 1870s; it became incorporated into the legal language of federal recognition to acknowledge the political relationship between a Nation and the United States.[11]

In 2021, the United States acknowledged that 574 federally recognized American Indian and Alaska Native tribal entities have certain inherent rights of self-government, as well as government-to-government relationships with the United States.[12] These sovereign nations have the responsibilities, powers, limitations, and obligations attached to that legal acknowledgment.

Federal recognition is the primary policy that affirms Tribes' existence as distinct political communities within the U.S. legal system. Federal recognition buffers tribal existence from most jurisdictional encroachments by state and local governments, and it is supposed to shield the Tribes from federal encroachments, as well. Furthermore, it provides Tribes and their members with certain political, legal, and economic rights. In contrast, Tribes without federal recognition have been marginalized. Consequently, they have experienced great difficulty sustaining themselves as viable political and cultural entities[13,14] and lack the resources to care for their members in times of crises (see the Epilogue of the book for a discussion on how Tribes without federal recognition have been affected by the COVID-19 pandemic.)

Unless a Tribe has federal recognition, it cannot be successful in exercising its inherent sovereign rights, including holding the federal government accountable for its trust obligations.[15] As already suggested in previous chapters, the federal recognition process is long, tedious, and expensive. However, it comes with significant advantages for Tribes and their members, so Tribes choose to undergo this process. When the process is successful, BIA programs support and assist federally recognized tribal entities in the development of their governments and strong economies, as well as quality programs to serve their members. BIA programs include services similar to those of state and local government, such as those for education, social services, law enforcement, courts, real-estate transactions, medical, agriculture, range management, and resource protection.[16] Tribes are also exempt from many state taxes, and individual tribal members also receive benefits because they have been legally defined as Native people.[17]

THE PROCESS OF FEDERAL RECOGNITION

"Asking a group of people who have been so persecuted to demonstrate that they've existed continuously through time is asking a lot." —Anonymous former DOI staff member[18]

Tracking the beginnings and evolution of the federal recognition process is difficult because of a multitude of factors. These include continuously changing terminology and the different avenues Tribes have available to them to pursue acknowledgment. The process is also difficult to successfully undertake without consulting those who have dealt directly with the process and succeeded. To humanize the long slog through this legal quagmire, three Native lawyers (who have dealt with the federal recognition process) were consulted for this book for assistance in gleaning the process from the Indigenous perspective. It also can translate the legal language of federal acknowledgment into something more comprehensible to individuals who are not lawyers.

In the 1870s, recognition began to be used in a jurisdictional sense.[19] However, it was not until the 1970s that a process was created to recognize Tribes that had historically maintained themselves as distinct communities. In other words, the full meaning of federal recognition was not clearly delineated for a very long time.

Basically, the federal recognition process requires an answer to the following multi-part question for Tribes to embark on it: Are you a sovereign tribal political entity, and does the government owe some kind of obligation to you, and/or is it giving you services based on that obligation?

At the end of the 1970s, the federal government tried to develop some consistency by creating related regulations that would ostensibly be consistently applied. As suggested previously in this book, the rules of the standard are difficult to meet.

Currently, the process has three basic steps.[20] First, a Tribe must send a Letter of Intent that it is going to petition for federal recognition. Second, the Office of Federal Recognition (OFA) responds to the Tribe with a letter assigning it a petitioner number. It is then up to the Tribe to file a completed petition, and there is no time limit. Generally, it will require a lawyer to compile the gathered evidence into a narrative that verifies that a Tribe meets the requirements of the regulations published at 25 CFR Part 83. As previously suggested in chapters 1–3, a positive determination of federal recognition demonstrates that a Tribe has proven that it meets a legal standard through the compilation of evidence.

However, the path to creating these rules has been complicated. Congress enacted Public Law 103-454 in 1994. The Federally Recognized Indian Tribe List Act[21] formally recognized three ways in which a Native group could become federally recognized.[22]

A digression to discuss the role of the courts is necessary at this juncture, since the courts are the usual way U.S. citizens expect legal disagreements to be decided. Because there is a formal administrative process for recognition, the courts have not shown any willingness to become involved in acknowledgment, however. For example, in 2001 in *Miami Nation of Indians of Indiana, Inc. v. United States Department of Interior*,[23] a ruling stated: "Recognition is, as we have pointed out, traditionally an executive function." On the other hand, if the Office of Federal Acknowledgement (OFA) violates a statute in its decision, or arbitrarily or capriciously denies acknowledging a petitioner under the Administrative Procedures Act, then a court could potentially order the OFA to acknowledge the Tribe.[24]

Instead of seeking legal redress in the courts, Native groups can petition through the Federal Acknowledgment Process (less formally known as the Administrative Process). Tribes can also seek recognition through the legislative process (via an act of Congress), by making a compelling case to the congressional representatives of the state in which they reside. It is important to note that Tribes that were terminated are barred from using the Federal Acknowledgment Process and can only be recognized through the legislative process. This is because only Congress can restore federal recognition to a terminated Tribe.[25]

The congressional representatives use the legislative process if they wish to do so. Whenever a bill fails to get enacted by the Congress in which it was introduced, it must start all over again with a new U.S. Congress. There is supposedly a path for Tribes to use a court process, but because of the administrative process, this has not actually been done.[26]

In 1978, the Secretary of the Interior created the regulations and administrative process giving Tribes the power to petition for federal acknowledgment. By the time the 1978 process came into being, there were 400 Tribes that were not federally recognized.[27] The BIA was tasked with administering the process.[28] However, it was not until 1979 that there was an official list of federally acknowledged Tribes.[29] The 1979 definition of Tribes seemed fairly straightforward; it called for the identification of the petitioners "from historical times until the present on a substantially continuous basis, as 'American Indian' or 'Aboriginal'" by the federal, state, or local governments, scholars or other Native tribes; the habitation of the tribes on the land identified as Indian; a functioning government that had authority over its members; a constitution; a roll of members based on criteria acceptable to the secretary of the interior; not being a terminated tribe; and members not belonging to other tribes.[30]

Within Regulation 25 CFR (of the legal code of federal regulations), Part 83 specifically required that Tribes meet the following seven criteria:

(1) that is has been from historical times until the present, on a continuous bases, identified as American Indian; (2) that a substantial portion of the group inhabits a specific area or lives in a community viewed as American Indian, distinct from other populations in the area; (3) that the group has maintained governmental authority over its members as an autonomous entity throughout history until the present; (4) that it provides a copy of its current governing documents including its membership criteria; (5) that the tribe's proven membership consists primarily of persons who are not members of any other Indian tribe; (6) that it submits a list of all known current members; and 7) that the tribe shows that the group has not been the subject of federal legislation expressly terminating its relationship with the U.S. government.[31]

However, this process was less straightforward for Tribes tasked with gathering the evidence than it should have been, so the criteria were updated in 2015, although it remains less straightforward than it initially can appear. The OFA was asked to provide clarification on some of the more complicated aspects of the process. However, after multiple tries, that information was not provided by Lee Fleming, Director of the Office of Acknowledgment. (The questions that Mr. Fleming sent are included in Appendix E.)

The BIA process was criticized for being too standardized, and because it homogenized Tribes it also ignored differences in social, cultural, and political organizations of Tribes to their detriment.[32,33] Legal code 25 CFR §83.11 was a 2015 update to recognition criteria and was meant to add transparency and fix through rewriting what many Tribes considered a broken process that included many consultations with Tribes. The goal of the revision was not to change the standard but to lower the evidentiary burden, as well as to define what was mandatory, according to the summary of 25 CFR §83.[34,35]

For example, the evidence collection time was moved forward. As noted in the Federal Register in 2015: "The Department does not classify the start date change from 1789, or the time of first sustained contact, to 1900, as a substantive change to the existing criteria."[36] The reasoning behind this included the following: the assimilation policies of the era, since some Tribes did not have sustained contact until the mid-1800s; because more records are available; because it provides a consistent start date; and because for the last forty years Tribes have been able to prove their existence onward from 1900.

Additionally, the land requirement changed to require evidence of a "distinct community," which is a broader term that has social ties within its meaning, as well as geographic ties.[37] The new criteria were also developed in response to the contemporary condition of Tribes seeking federal recognition. The changes to the federal final rule state:

1) The Department implemented 1900 as a start date for the evaluation of criterion (a) to reduce the documentary burden of this criterion while retaining the requirement for substantially continuous identification as an Indian entity. The rule defined "historical" as prior to 1900. Using pre-1900 for the end date of "historical" and 1900 for the start date for analysis of community and political influence/authority allows for a rigorous and seamless examination of each petitioner, requiring evidence of descent from a historical Indian tribe that existed prior to 1900 and requiring an evaluation of identification, community, and political influence/authority for more than a century from 1900 to the present.[38]
2) The final rule also retains the current requirement that a criterion be met "without substantial interruption."

3) The final rule maintains the current standard of proof as "reasonable likelihood" without judicial explanations of the phrase.
4) The final rule doesn't allow for limited re-petitioning.

Notably, in addition to the racist laws that attempted to erase the existence of Indigenous people, there were times when it was not safe for a Tribe to keep any evidence that it was behaving like a Tribe. Consequently, some Tribes have had difficulty collecting the required records for documentation and the amount of documentation required has increased, as well.

Anthropologists, genealogists, historians, and lawyers are required to gather the evidence. This evidence includes birth and death records, meeting notices, and minutes that demonstrate community and political autonomy. The process of gathering the material as well as OFA process of analyzing the evidence takes a very long time. That high standard for the analysis is purported to protect the sanctity of what it means to be federally recognized, by continuing to "maintain the integrity and substantive rigor of the process."[39] According to the former DOI staff member interviewed for this research, "an administrative precedent developed that raised the bar about evidence allowable to meet the criteria."

According to Locklear, the first submitted petitions were only around 100 pages in total; Tribes could do it themselves with volunteers who were historians, academics, and others interested in helping, but over time the petitions grew ever lengthier such that after ten to fifteen years there was growing pressure from those who processed the petitions to make them more detailed and technical.

At this point, the Tribes were no longer able to complete the petitions with solely volunteer assistance. As Locklear stated, "It's only because the federal government made it so hard that Tribes could no longer do it on their own that gaming stepped in to fill the [financial] gap." Presently, without significant pro bono legal help, a petition cannot be completed by the Tribe itself, unless a Tribe is backed by the money of the gaming industry. (The history of the gaming industry and income generated by it is discussed in detail in chapter 12.)

If a Tribe wanted to appeal a negative decision on a completed petition under the old regulations, it would need to go through the Interior Board of Indian Appeals (aka the Board). The Board's jurisdiction to review final acknowledgment determinations was limited to reviewing the grounds upon which the Board could either affirm the Assistant Secretary's determination or vacate and remand to the Assistant Secretary for further work and reconsideration[40] A petitioning Tribe had to establish that: (1) there was new evidence, (2) that most of the prior evidence was unreliable, (3) that the prior research was inadequate or incomplete, and/or (4) there was alternative interpretations of the evidence. This was a tremendous hurdle. And, once a Tribe was denied, it could not petition again.

The new regulations (2015) eliminated the appeal review by the Board and now only allows petitioners to seek a hearing before an Office of Hearings and Appeals judge. There is another path for recognition called "reaffirmation," but the DOI does not consider reaffirmation the same as acknowledgment governed by the Part 83 process. Instead, the DOI considers reaffirmation as resulting from "separate contexts and were made after a rigorous review of the unique facts and circumstances of each Native group on a case-by-case basis."[41] Reaffirmation only rarely occurred, and it is no longer available since the adoption of the new regulations in 2015.[42]

STATE RECOGNITION AND TRIBES WITHOUT RECOGNITION

Only thirteen states have officially state-recognized Tribes.[43] Most of those are in the southeastern geographic area of the United States. These state-recognized (versus federally recognized) Tribes are located in Alabama, Connecticut, Delaware, Georgia, Louisiana, Maryland, Massachusetts, New Jersey, New York, North Carolina, South Carolina, Vermont, and Virginia. State recognition does not necessarily lead to, nor is it a prerequisite for, federal recognition, although the BIA does consider a historical relationship between Tribes and state in the federal recognition determination for the criteria of historical habitation in a specific place.

Virginia had only state-recognized Tribes until 2015. The Pamunkey Tribe, recognized through the BIA's Federal Acknowledgment Process (FAP) in 2015, was the first Tribe in Virginia to receive federal recognition. Six additional Virginia Tribes received recognition through the legislative route after giving up on the BIA process. In January 2018, U.S. Senators Tim Kaine (D-Va.) and Mark Warner (D-Va.) secured the final passage of the Thomasina E. Jordan Indian Tribes of Virginia Federal Recognition Act of 2017. Signed by President Trump, the legislation granted federal recognition to the Chickahominy Indian Tribe, the Chickahominy Indian Tribe-Eastern Division, the Upper Mattaponi Tribe, the Rappahannock Tribe, the Monacan Indian Nation, and the Nansemond Indian Tribe. This is the first time such a bill made it past the Senate phase to garner enactment, although both U.S. Senators and House members from Virginia had pushed for Virginia-based Tribes' federal recognition since the 1990s. Senators George Allen and John Warner first introduced the legislation in the Senate in 2002.[44]

Although disregarded by federal and state governments, many other Tribes continue to exist as contemporary Tribes and practice their cultures, languages, and traditional governments. Many of these Tribes do not meet the stereotypical image and expectations of already recognized Tribes under either the old or the new recognition criteria. Additionally, other barriers, many of them rooted in white supremacist race-based structures, make the federal recognition petitions process far more grueling than necessary.

But the process of federal recognition is an important part of tribal sovereignty. However, while Tribes need to be federally recognized to benefit from the sovereign relationship afforded by such acknowledgment, racist laws that disempower Indigenous people and other people of color have often thwarted their ability to gain what should be legally accessible to them. The seven latest Tribes in Virginia to receive recognition were all victims of this racist system. Empowering Native people, or any people of color, is the opposite of what white supremacist U.S. leaders sought to accomplish, so the hurdles were their way of maintaining their own top-tier level of power. In other words, a white hegemonic system of power places the burden of proof on the Tribes amid a backdrop of racist laws and stereotypical images. This is the lived reality of Indigenous peoples and their Tribes. First, Tribes that petition for federal recognition have always had history working against them. Second, racist laws from Jim Crow to eugenics erased Tribes and their individual members. Third, stereotypical images promoted by mass media foiled efforts at recognition by non-Plains Tribes and/or when tribal members didn't have the appearance of Indians expected by the white elites holding governmental leadership roles.

The creators of assimilationist policies at the federal government level mostly hoped that Tribes would have disappeared a long time ago. The Tribes of Virginia is just an example of Indigenous Nations affected by these damaging policies.

JIM CROW AND THE RACIAL INTEGRITY ACT OF VIRGINIA

The government hoped that the Removal Era of the 1830s through 1840s would eliminate any Indians left in the South. But many Southeastern Tribes were not actually considered a threat because they held so little land, and racial segregation was strictly enforced to ensure privilege for whites only. Thus, these Tribes became an invisible part of black and white society, but not invisible enough, so laws were enacted to try to get rid of Indians once and for all.

The 1924 Racial Integrity Act and two other "racial integrity" laws were designed to protect the United States as a "white" nation by preventing racial intermixing that could produce mixed-race offspring. Under the direction of Dr. Walter Plecker, the Bureau of Vital Statistics divided Virginians into strictly defined racial categories of "white" and "colored"; banning intermarriage between people of different races was legalized. White people with less than 1/16 Native blood (as long as they were not mixed with any other race) could be classified as white.[45]

The Public Assemblages Act of 1926 made all public meeting spaces strictly segregated. Legislation that codified "Colored persons and Indians defined" was enacted in 1930, as exemplified by the following passage:

> Every person in whom there is ascertainable any negro blood shall be deemed and taken to be a colored person, and every person not a colored person having one-fourth or more of American Indian blood shall be deemed an American Indian; except that members of Indian tribes living on reservations allotted them by the Commonwealth of Virginia having one-fourth or more of Indian blood and less than one-sixteenth of negro blood shall be deemed tribal Indians so long as they are domiciled on said reservations.[46]

This "one drop rule" occurred concurrently with the promotion of eugenics (a white supremacist theory) that was gaining support from groups, such as the Anglo-Saxon Clubs of America. These groups believed that the mixing of races in the United States could cause great societal harm, even though the races had been intermixed since European settlement.[47] Among the group's goals was "the preservation and maintenance of Anglo-Saxon ideals and civilization, the intelligent selection and exclusion of immigrants, and the final solutions of our racial problems . . . most especially . . . the negro problem."[48]

Plecker regulated the racial classifications of Virginians and was concerned blacks were attempting to pass as white. The goal of racial integrity was to eliminate any legal recognition of their status as Indians and categorize them as "colored."[49] The legal classification of most Natives as "colored" (but some "white") gave Plecker the impetus to take action to erase Virginia's Indians, which would eliminate the future possibility of their acquiring self-determination. Tribes could not prove their historical existence if all Indians were reclassified as non-Indian, but proving Native existence is required in federal-recognition criteria.

Only in 1967 was the Racial Integrity Act finally overturned. However, it took another thirty years for the Virginia General Assembly[50] to condemn the Act (as well as eugenics) as racist in intent.[51]

Still remaining are historical records generated during the time of the Racial Integrity Act's enforcement, such as birth, marriage, and death certificates, which classified tribal members as white or colored. Long after Plecker's time in office ceased, his successor would continue to write on the backs of birth certificates that the individual's grandparents had been married as "colored."⁵² After the Racial Integrity Act was repealed, "for a fee, Indians could receive a copy of their birth certificate listing their race as Indian, with the 'Plecker note' removed from the back."⁵³ House Bill (HB2889) in 1997 eventually did allow the records to be changed free of charge.⁵⁴

Meanwhile, other seemingly minor policies play a role in making it difficult for Tribes to collect the evidence needed for the administrative process.

THE ROLE OF THE U.S. CENSUS IN ELIMINATING INDIANS

The Census of 1850 was the first to include information on American Indian demographics. Estimates of populations were gathered from reports from the Indian Office (the American States Papers) and information included a one-page summary of the Indian population for the years 1789, 1825, and 1853. Exemplifying the goal of eliminating Native peoples, the Louisiana population of Natives was left blank for the year 1853.⁵⁵ The Census table includes a note stating, "It is believed that there are but few Indians now in Louisiana."

It is likely that the census takers in the South disregarded Natives who had intermarried with blacks and simply categorized them as black due to the codification of racist policies. In 1864, U.S. Marshals, who were the census-takers, were tasked with determining the "status" of each Indian counted. The Marshal had the authority to decide whether the person had renounced tribal rule and exercised the rights of a citizen. If so, then that individual should be included in the total population with a notation of "Ind."⁵⁶ By the 1900s the government was an expert in eliminating Indians: "In 1900, enumerators were instructed to record the fraction of White ancestry ('blood') possessed by each American Indian, his or her Tribe, and the tribes of his or her mother and father. This presaged the introduction of hyperdescent rules for American Indians. These rules would establish lower bounds of ancestry, below which individuals could not legally claim to be recognized as an American Indian . . . hyperdescent was a convenient device for limiting the obligations from treaties and other agreements that had been incurred by the federal government throughout the preceding century."⁵⁷

Each of these methods of counting the population for the Census provided additional mechanisms to reduce the total Native population. Stereotypical phenotypical notions of Native identity furthered the process of an incorrectly reduced count. "True Indians," in the eyes of the dominant culture holding the power, are static, historical figures. Nothing else. In their perspective, authentic Indians have not changed since first contact with non-Indians. In other words, "Indians who had assimilated into modern society" emerged in white eyes as "negative others,"⁵⁸ but were not truly Indian. This notion of authenticity has not significantly changed in centuries, but it has biased the general public's understanding of federal recognition if they have heard of it at all. The mainstream media (both news and cultural) are not immune to the authenticity stereotype and has perpetuated false ideas and images of Indians throughout the U.S. history. Journalists have also been duped by such false narratives, such as the centrality of casinos to Native culture and essence, which just fosters heightened misperceptions and beliefs about current issues facing Indigenous peoples and Tribes.

NOTES

1. Chapter 576 of the 73rd Congress, Approved June 18, 1934, 48 Stat. 984, 25 U.S.C. 461 et seq.
2. 25 U.S.C. § 461.
3. Osburn, 2009. Tribes do update their membership criteria, so references may be outdated.
4. Wilkins, 2005; House Resolution 108 reads: "That it is declared to be the sense of Congress that, at the earliest possible time, all of the Indian tribes and the individual members thereof located within the States of California, Florida, New York, and Texas, and all of the following named Indian tribes and individual members thereof, should be freed from Federal supervision and control and from all disabilities and limitations specially applicable to Indians: The Flathead Tribe of Montana, the Klamath Tribe of Oregon, the Menominee Tribe of Wisconsin, the Potowatamie Tribe of Kansas and Nebraska, and those members of the Chippewa Tribe that are on the Turtle Mountain Reservation, North Dakota. It is further declared to be the sense of Congress that, upon the release of such tribes and individual members thereof from such disabilities and limitations, all offices of the Bureau of Indian Affairs in the States of California, Florida, New York, and Texas and all other offices of the Bureau of Indian Affairs whose primary purpose was to serve any Indian tribe or individual Indian freed from Federal supervision should be abolished."
5. Pevar, 2004.
6. Getches, Wilkinson, & Williams, 2005.
7. Kelly, 2010.
8. Wilkins & Stark, 2011.
9. Wilkins & Stark, 2011.
10. Arlinda Locklear interview.
11. Wilkins & Stark, 2011.
12. See the U.S. *Federal Register*, 2021 for more details of this change.
13. McCulloch & Wilkins, 1995.
14. Pevar, 2002.
15. However, there are some exceptions. For example, in *Joint Tribal Council of the Passamaquoddy Tribe v. Morton*, 528 F.2d 370 (1st Cir. 1975), the Passamaquoddy sued the United States seeking to force the United States to exercise its trust responsibility and defend the tribe's land. The Passamaquoddy were not yet

federally recognized, and the United States' defense was essentially that there is no trust responsibility to Tribes that are not federally recognized. The First Circuit sided with the Tribe, saying that federal recognition was the acknowledgment of a trust responsibility, but that lack of federal recognition did not necessarily mean that there was no trust responsibility.

16. More information regarding the range of *BIA* services can be acquired from the website of the U.S. Department of the Interior, Tribal Nations Benefits and Service (see: www.doi.gov/tribe/benefits).

17. Wilkins and Stark, 2011.

18. The former staff member was interviewed on March 16, 2021, and was asked to remain anonymous due to the individual's current professional position. The publisher has been provided with that information.

19. Quinn, 1990, p. 362 states "a series of a series of judicial decisions in the mid-1970s in motivating the Department of the Interior to adopt a uniform procedure and standard criteria for recognizing unrecognized Indian tribes."

20. The process of federal recognition is codified in 25 CFR §§ 83.20-83.22.

21. 108 Stat. 4791, 4792.

22. For the current exact language of the three rules, see the BIA website (www.bia.gov/FAQs/).

23. *Miami Nation of Indians of Indiana, Inc. v. United States Department of the Interior*, 255 F.3d 342, 346 (7th Cir. 2001).

24. Courts will determine whether the decision was arbitrary and capricious, whether the agency abused its discretion, or whether the decision was not made in accordance with the law. *Id. See also* 5 U.S.C. § 706.

25. A Chinook Indian Nation lawsuit is currently challenging this law. See Whitford, 2021.

26. Dan Lewerenz (Iowa Tribe of Kansas and Nebraska)—who is a staff attorney for the Native American Rights Fund in the DC office and former president of the Native American Journalists Association—worked as an attorney advisor in the U.S. DIA's Division of Indian Affairs. He stated that theoretically a Tribe could make their case to a court. However, he did not know of any instances where a Tribe has received its U.S. recognition by the courts.

27. For the names of these Tribes, see: the U.S. Government Accountability Office's "Indian Issues" (1991). A separate process exists for acknowledging Native Hawaiians; for info on Native Hawaiians, see the federal publication, *Frequently Asked Questions on Part 50—The Final Ruling for Procedures Reestablishing a Formal Government to-Government Relationship with the Native Hawaiian Community* (published Sept. 2016) (www.doi.gov/sites/doi.gov/files/uploads/external_faqs_on_part_50_final_rule_9.21.16_final.pdf).

28. See legal code: 25 CFR §83 Procedures for Federal Acknowledgment of Indian Tribes.

29. Quinn, 1990.

30. See legal code: 25 CFR 83.7 What Are the Criteria for Acknowledgment as a Federally Recognized Tribe?

31. See 25 C.F.R. §83.7 Mandatory Criteria for Federal Acknowledgment.

32. McCulloch & Wilkins, 1995.
33. Pevar, 2002.
34. The summary of the proposed rule states that the revisions under 25 CFR Part 83 aimed "to make the process and criteria more transparent, promote consistent implementation, and increase timeliness and efficient, while maintain the integrity of the process." https://www.bia.gov/sites/bia.gov/files/assets/as-ia/opa/pdf/idc1-026772.pdf. It goes on to state that "[t]he proposed rule would reform the process by, among other things, institutionalizing a phased review that allows for faster decisions; reducing the documentary burden; allowing for a hearing on the proposed finding to promote transparency and process integrity; establishing the Assistant Secretary's final determination as final for the Department to promote efficiency; and establishing objective standards, where appropriate, to ensure transparency and predictability." *Id*.
35. I contacted Lee Fleming, head of the office of Federal Recognition to get further clarity on the acknowledgment process after a completed petition is submitted. He did call me back and asked me to send him questions via email. Those questions were submitted, and he told me that a meeting was being convened on May 3, 2021 to answer those questions. However, he never responded. I have put the questions I was hoping he would answer in *Appendix F*.
36. See: Legal Code 25 CFR §83.7, Mandatory Criteria for Federal Acknowledgment, 80 FR pages 37861-37895
37. See: Legal Code 25 CFR §83.11 What are the Criteria for Acknowledgment as a Federally Recognized Tribe?
38. Federal Acknowledgment of American Indian Tribes, A Rule by the Bureau of Indian Affairs on July 1, 2015.
39. See U.S. Legal Code Executive Summary 25 CFR §83.
40. See Legal Code 25 CFR §83 (d)(1)-(4)).
41. Newland, 2012 "The Department does not consider these actions to constitute 'acknowledgement' of an Indian tribe in the manner governed by the Part 83 process. Rather, these actions were undertaken in separate contexts, and were made after a rigorous review of the unique facts and circumstances of each tribe on a case-by-case basis."
42. Between 1973 and 2009, thirty-eight Tribes that had been terminated were restored. See: GAO report number GAO-12-348, *Indian Issues: Federal Funding for Non-Federally Recognized Tribes*; May 9, 2012. "This appendix provides information about tribes whose relationship with the United States was terminated. These tribes are not eligible to petition for federal recognition through the Department of the Interior's administrative acknowledgement process but may have their recognition restored by other means." (p. 36)
43. National Conference of State Legislators, 2020.
44. Schilling, 2018.
45. Wolfe, 2015.
46. Virginia State Law. Supplement to the Virginia Legal Code, 1926, pp. 42–43.
47. Wolfe, 2015.
48. Smith, 1993.
49. Wolfe, 2015.

50. The Virginia General Assembly is the legislative body of the Commonwealth of Virginia, established on July 30, 1619, it is the oldest continuous law-making body in the Americas.

51. Wolfe, 2015.
52. Roundtree, 1996.
53. Waugaman & Moretti-Langholtz, 2000, p. 33.
54. See, http://lis.virginia.gov/cgi-bin/legp604.exe?971+sum+HB2889.
55. U.S. Bureau of the Census data, 1853.
56. Jobe, 2004.
57. Snipp, 2003, p. 568.
58. Deloria, 1998.

Chapter 4

Hegemony, Framing, and Agenda Setting in Indian Country

> Mainstream journalism . . . has been nearly the only source of widely available information and open discussion on gaming and racial identity.[1]

Tribal sovereignty is misunderstood by most Americans. Therefore, it follows that mainstream media reporters and editors are also ignorant of it.[2] Sovereignty is not taught in American schools. And, unless journalism students happen to have a Native professor, or take classes in Indigenous studies, it is doubtful that they are even aware of it. Tribal sovereignty is also misunderstood by high-level government officials. In a famous interview at the Unity, Journalists of Color Convention in 2004, Mark Trahant, a reporter and former president of the Native American Journalists Association, asked U.S. President George W. Bush what the meaning of tribal sovereignty in the twenty-first century meant. Astoundingly, Bush replied, "Tribal sovereignty means that. It's sovereign. You're a . . . you're a . . . you've been given sovereignty and you're viewed as a sovereign entity."[3]

Elementary schools in the United States include lessons about Indians, but seldom challenge racist historical accounts or discuss contemporary Indian issues. The same is true for high schools. Instead, Native people are typically portrayed as historical stereotypes; only Native American or American Indian Studies Department college courses provide the basics of tribal authority and tribal systems of governments. A 2015 study examining the standards for teaching Native American history and culture in all fifty states found that 87 percent of references about Native Americans are in a pre-1900s context.[4] This study also found:

- In half of the states, no individual Natives or specific Tribes are named.
- Of the Natives named in standards, the most common are Sacagawea, Squanto, Sequoyah, and Sitting Bull.

- Only sixty-two Native Nations are named in standards; most are mentioned by only one state. (One Nation, the Iroquois, is mentioned in six states.)
- Only four states—Arizona, Washington, Oklahoma, and Kansas—include content about Indian boarding schools.
- New Mexico is the only state to mention, by name, a member of the American Indian Movement.
- Washington is the only state to use the word "genocide" in relation to Natives. That word is used in the standards for fifth-grade U.S. history.
- Nebraska textbooks portray Natives as lazy, drunk, or criminal.
- Ninety percent of all manuscripts written about Native people are authored by non-Native writers.

The U.S. education system, like mainstream media, is meant to reflect the social order of those who hold power—white, economically elite males. This is how institutionalized racism is perpetuated. Those same white economic elites were formally educated in a system that is steeped in racist stereotypes, such that students acquire an understanding of Indigenous people as relics of the past. Likewise, these mainly white journalists who were educated in a racist system are responsible for reporting and editing most of the mainstream news that informs the public.

News media play a significant role in the way people perceive the world and other people, and especially people that are not part of a majority culture's "in-groups."

Longstanding research on belief and personality systems suggests people's attitudes and opinions can be altered by credible and trustworthy sources.[5] Both conservative and liberal news media outlets are viewed as reliable and present sound reporting, so citizens holding viewpoints across the ideological political spectrum can be influenced by news media reports.[6] News media portrayals have shaped public opinion and public policy for Native people since the first images of Indians appeared centuries ago. There can be no doubt that centuries of inaccurate, stereotypical, and biased news reports have produced a flawed and widespread public impression that continues to adversely impact the lives of Native people today.

ROLE OF THE NEWS MEDIA AND THEIR INFLUENCE ON POLITICS: HEGEMONY, FRAMING, AND AGENDA SETTING

What constitutes "the news" is a version of reality decided by journalistic norms along with prevailing attitudes as to what is "newsworthy." The news media (e.g., newspapers, broadcast, web-based outlets, and television) construct and present a pseudo-environment that shapes how the public views the world.[7] As the frame-makers of this reality, and through the agenda-setting role they play in society, the news media have a significant effect on public opinion and the debate that goes into policymaking. Because the mainstream media are largely staffed by privileged, white people who have less direct experience with racism than people of color in the United States, the media also reinforces the hegemonic dominance of the white status quo for groups with very little political power.[8]

Previous research defines the news media as a major means by which a dominant ideology is circulated to and accepted by subordinate groups.[9,10,11,12,13] Other studies have shown that, although news routinely emphasizes meanings and values associated with groups who hold institutional power, they also indicate what will challenge it.[14] Furthermore—although coverage is denied to no one—it is difficult to obtain by some groups.[15] Overall, coverage supports the existing sources of power in the culture, and people of color are predominantly framed in three ways: traditional stereotypes, outside the norm, or not at all.

Agenda setting and framing research show how news can influence audiences through the choice of what stories to feature and how much importance to give particular features within those reports.[16] It is through the selection of particular issue attributes that news affects public opinion.[17]

Agenda setting is a theory about the transfer of salience from the mass media's perspective to the audience's perspective; the media set the public's agenda because the degree of emphasis placed on issues influences the priority accorded to them by the public.[18] Previous research has identified certain performative roles that help determine media's ability to set the agenda.[19] That agenda setting includes conflict or drama around an issue; valence and effect, such as spurring negative emotions, which can mobilize people to become politically active; and article placement. In other words, agenda setting occurs due to the frequency with which an issue is covered in the mass media, and how a social issue is framed by the mass media can make a difference in how the public responds to it.

For example, prior research has shown that the news media impose the norms of campaign coverage (i.e., the type of news coverage generally used in electing officials); that imposition occurs in varied policy debates, and that this type of news coverage minimizes the public's ability to understand the full context of these debates.[20,21] News can support or challenge policymakers, and thereby affect the policies they are trying to advance. Those trying to influence public officials as well as the officials themselves attempt to advance their policy perspectives and preferences through the media.[22,23,24,25] Coverage of Indigenous people and communities and the issues that concern them are affected by both agenda setting and framing, and particularly because of the absence of coverage of Native people and issues, in general.

Media framing refers to the way events and issues are organized and made sense of by media professionals and their audiences.[26] Story frames make pieces of news information more memorable, noticeable, and meaningful.[27,28] Frames also provide journalists with models based on newsworthiness for the quick selection, emphasis, and presentation in their covering of events/issues within a given news story, and whether the journalists are conscious of them or not.[29,30,31,32] Framing theory suggests that the mass media not only help audiences understand an issue but shape the public's interpretation of those issues.[33]

Societal and group frames are inculcated via shared educational and media images and become part of culture. For Indigenous people and their cultures, these frames encompass and transfer the myths, stereotypes, attitudes, beliefs, values, and behaviors shared by the dominant white society.[34] The media have framed Native people to reflect the needs of colonial Europe beginning with the first contact. Journalistic frames of Indigenous people have continuously morphed to ensure these journalistic frames reflect the needs of the white hegemony. Generally speaking, the frames are designed to ignore Natives and their issues because Indigenous groups are "un-people"[35]—and "un-people" are easier to report on in ways that are sensationalized and anachronistic, and in ways that lack cultural and historical context, because they are not considered relevant.[36,37,38] This lack of relevance often equates to invisibility in the news agenda.

Public attention on the "news" decreases over time. For this reason, the news media must deal with its quickly changing interests by focusing on episodic frames over thematic frames. Episodic frames concentrate attention on specific events or cases. They tend to focus audience attention on events in the lives of individuals, often blaming these individuals for their plight. In contrast, thematic frames place political issues and events into context, and tend to place blame with governmental or political actors. The news media, as an agenda setter, can move issues on and off the policy agenda. Likewise, journalists can decide to frame stories episodically or thematically. Thus, the news media influence the attention of policymakers toward particular issues, through public response to journalistic reporting of those issues. The news media are very effective in producing symbolic responses from policymakers by using these journalistic conventions, but the public expects the stories to solve a problem.[39] Because the media are involved at each policymaking stage: problem formation; agenda setting; policy formation, legitimatization and adoption; implementation; administration; and evaluation, they can impact it at any stage. Moreover, ideologies funneled through the media are likely to emphasize the "legitimacy of the state and established class institutions, delegitimating of challenges to the social order, and discontent and frustration towards non-conformists."[40] It is a mechanism that reinforces ideologies and supports those who the dominant culture view as virtuous and useful and disavows those who are dangerous or inadequate.[41]

Natives have almost always been considered inadequate and, at numerous times, dangerous. Contemporary images of Indians conceptualize them as "bad actors." This supersedes the other, longstanding, and second-most held, image of helpless victims taking advantage of federal laws to enrich themselves at the expense of taxpayers. Federal policymakers have been successful at pushing these stereotypes onto the news media.[42] Notably, the "bad Indian" image overtakes the "Indian victim" when financial resources of the dominant culture are at stake. This pattern has repeated itself in different variations for more than 300 years.

HISTORY OF FRAMES WITH INDIAN STEREOTYPES ARISE

Ethnic slurs and stereotypes against Indians initially appeared in American English when the first British colonists encountered the Indigenous people of the East Coast of North America. The earliest appearance of the term "redskin" was in 1699. It was one of the first racial slurs applied to Indians by white settlers. Indeed, many references to Natives include statements that refer to "barbarous Indians," who are found "lurking about" and/or are "sculking."[43] Other commonly held stereotypes included the "heathen war-like savage" that was created by the frontiersmen who had to justify taking land from the Native people occupying it.[44] Yet another stereotype that often appeared in written commentary, such as editorials in newspapers, was the "noble red man"; this originated with such European writers as Montaigne, Shakespeare, and Rousseau.[45] Scalping also became part of this image—although the practice was unknown among Native people until 1637 when colonists began to offer cash for the heads of their enemies and later accepted just scalps.[46]

Preconceptions of Indigenous culture were also important in shaping attitudes toward Indians. The English and other Europeans held the Indians in contempt, as their policies were directed at controlling, civilizing, and exterminating Indians. By the first half of the eighteenth century, the "threat" from Indians was receding. Therefore, the "ignoble" image of the Indian gave rise to the "noble savage." Although appearing to offer a way of looking at Indians in terms of their own cultural worth, the reality was that this did not change the non-Native attitude that placed Native people and culture as impeding "civilization." This type of status-based prejudice, anchored in negative personal experience and driven by status policies, is very resistant to change.[47] These prejudices reflected the colonial belief system; therefore, these beliefs were replicated in the existent colonial "media."

One of the functions of the mass media is the production and transformation of the above-described beliefs or ideologies. Ideology refers to "those images, concepts and premises which provide the frameworks through which we represent, interpret, understand and make sense of some aspect of social existence."[48] These representations are often false, and especially in depicting people of color. Moreover, these racist ideologies became ingrained in conventional wisdom, and they worked to maintain the ideology of superiority of white European settlers over the Indigenous people, which persists in the prejudices of white supremacists toward people of color to the present time.

Robert Berkhofer's book—*The White Man's Indian* (1978)[49]—was considered groundbreaking in terms of images and stereotypes of Native people; it is still relevant forty years later. Berkhofer defined three persistent practices found throughout the history of white interpretation of Natives. These are the following: (1) generalizing from one tribe's society and culture to all Indians (and all tribes); (2) conceiving of Indians in terms of their deficiencies according to white ideals, rather than in terms of their own various cultures; and (3) using moral evaluation as the prevailing description of Indians. It is essential to realize that these practices have not changed since the first appearance of the term "redskin," and they have proliferated through the norms and functions of news production in both framing and agenda setting.

News Coverage of Native Americans

Academic research has reinforced what Indigenous people have argued since the first news stories about Indians appeared: that they are not newsworthy, so are generally absent in the media unless they become a challenge to social norms.[50]

Research on people of color in the news media has generally examined coverage that reinforces racial stereotypes, multicultural celebrations, and the effect of coverage when an attempt at racial parity is made. Research on the coverage of Indigenous people in the news media is not much different, but there certainly is very little of it. Unless search terms are used that specifically seek out stories on issues or events concerning Indigenous people and their cultures, such research is difficult to locate because of the dearth of news stories about them.

The first comprehensive analysis was Mary Ann Weston's book titled *Native Americans in the News*.[51] Weston examined newspaper coverage of Native American issues that dominated each decade from 1920 to 1990. Her book analyzed the perceptions that news consumers form based on newspaper and magazine articles, and how those perceptions affect public perception and public policy. She concluded that, although Natives are ubiquitous in America, "Native Americans are virtually invisible."[52] Thirty years later, the book has not been updated, but the perceptions have not changed, and Indians are still invisible.

John M. Coward conducted a comprehensive study of the portrayal of conflicts between American Indians and whites in the nineteenth century and how that contributed to ideas about hostile Indians. Coward concluded that Indigenous identity in the nineteenth-century press was confined to the ideology of civilization and progress, where Indian people were considered primarily as obstacles to economic growth and national development.[53] This is still true in twenty-first-century news outlets.

The 2002 *Reading Red Report* (conducted by the Native American Journalists Association) analyzed articles appearing from 1999 to 2001, and from nine of the largest circulation newspapers in the United States. "The best stories simply reflected good-quality and fair-minded reporting; writing and editing applied to Native America. They treated Native Americans as people rather than historical figures. But, most stories failed to accurately represent Indian Country."[54]

As an edited collection of contributed chapters, *American Indians and the Mass Media*[55] illustrates the impact of media upon American Indian cultures, histories, and communities from a wide variety of viewpoints. Meanwhile, there are other collections that have focused on the coverage of people of color, in general, but with an included analysis of coverage of Indigenous people from different perspectives.

For example, *White News*[56] noted in local television news coverage the "news workers' orientation to the world may have precluded some stories from being covered, and that a lack of knowledge of basic history of Native Americans and their issues created a barrier between sources and news gatherers. Additionally, local television news does not cover Native Americans because they are considered part of the 'past' as opposed to the 'present.'"

News for All the People: The Epic Story of Race and the American Media[57] examines specific portrayals (such as the "skulking Indian") from the time of the first colonies; it also finds little change in coverage over time, as eventually Indians get pushed further from mainstream coverage and only appear in news because of a specific event. For example, in 1993 the emergence of a new strain of Hantavirus in the United States was reported. It fostered a variety of negative and stereotypical reporting on the Navajo people. Terms such as "Navajo flu," "Indian ailment," and "Navajo disease" were casually used in the mainstream media.

Subsequently, the 2005 shootings on the Red Lake Reservation in Minnesota caught journalists off guard. It was difficult for mainstream reporters to get access to reservation residents as sources because of their estranged relationship with the news media. Erick Black, a reporter for the Red Lake Net News, noted that no news anchors turned up to cover the event; however, the *New York Times* published three front-page stories in one week. A quantitative content analysis found that the reporting of Red Lake focused on race and class, compared to the shootings at Columbine in 1999.[58] Another study analyzed the use of the internet by Indigenous media outlets to cover the Red Lake story, and found that—while the Internet has changed the role of Native media outlets—both the printed and electronic Native American media maintain their relevance by providing news by and for Native Americans.[59] That study concluded that the non-Native journalists do not understand the sovereignty of Tribes leading to further misinterpretations between Natives and non-Natives,[60] and that Native journalists strive to explain "the political relationships of tribal nations to the federal government, i.e. sovereignty, as well as historical context."[61]

The 2002 *Reading Red Report* analyzed 1,133 articles appearing from 1999 to 2001 from nine of the largest circulation newspapers in the United States at the time.[62] Most stories did not portray Native people in their breadth of experiences. Mascot team names, gaming and "On the Res" stories made up most of the topics. The 2007 *Reading Red Report* examined if newspapers in circulation areas with high percentages of Native Americans fairly and accurately covered Indian Country.[63] Just over 7 percent of the 1,867 stories analyzed were found to be casino stories, which constituted the third-most common topic. Both of the *Reading Red Reports* reported that most of the stories about Natives were arts and entertainment articles. Overall, almost 75 percent of the sources in all the articles examined were non-Native. The report did not note how the percent of Native and non-Native sources in casino stories were determined.

More recently, the Dakota Access Pipeline (DAPL) brought attention to the lives of Indigenous people to greater media attention. The construction project for the pipeline was announced in 2014, when residents of Standing Rock Reservation (Sioux) rapidly attracted public attention because of their opposition to its construction. However, construction work began in April 2016; and the Sioux of the Standing Rock Reservation created the Sacred Stone Camp to protest in proximity to the planned path of the pipeline.

The "Water Protectors" demanded the rerouting of the DAPL because of the danger to the water supply (the Missouri River) and geographic area they held sacred. The number of protesters grew rapidly. The No DAPL movement represented the largest gathering of Indigenous Tribes in more than 100 years.[64] The No DAPL activists strategically used social media to get their message out. Each activist camp created dedicated accounts on Twitter, Instagram, and Facebook providing constant updates. Indigenous journalists also used news websites, such as Indian Country Today Media Network and Indigenous Rising Media.[65] Eventually, the mainstream media could no longer ignore the story.

A recent framing analysis of the Standing Rock movement coverage found that the frames employed by each news outlet differed by type and frequency. Ellen Moore's book in 2018—*Journalism, Politics, and the Dakota Access Pipeline*[66]—identified frames to understanding how journalists or news agencies chose to present the Indigenous struggle over the DAPL. The DAPL analysis included more than 550 articles from three U.S. and three Canadian news sources: The *New York Times*, the *Bismarck Tribune* (which accounted for almost 75 percent of the articles), *Indian Country Media Network*, *National Post*, the *Globe and Mail*, and the *Calgary Herald*.

The *Indian Country Media Network* provided historical context for the issue and gave primacy to Indigenous voices and perspectives during the struggle. The *New York Times* adopted an environmental justice frame "losing some of its adherence to the professional standard of 'balance' for a cause it thought was justified."[67] In comparison, Moore's study found that The *Bismarck Tribune*, while at times utilizing the lens of environmental justice, employed the language and rhetoric of "law and order," and framed the protesters as a threat to the social fabric.

The research points to the location of the mainstream media outlets as what possibly accounted for the differences in framing. The *New York Times* did not overtly seem to have any stake in the outcome of its reporting. However, the *Bismarck Tribune* is based in both a state and geographical region reliant on fossil fuels exploration. North Dakota's economy experienced a revival because of fracking and the ability to transport the oil out of state. The study concluded that the *New York Times* was willing to be critical of the oil industry for what it perceived to be injustice, the *Bismarck Tribune* was not. The analysis presented found that focus of the three Canadian newspaper stories were on the potential impact of the Canadian "oil patch" and its related industries.

Another study analyzing online The *New York Times* and Fox News stories of the No DAPL found that both news organizations framed the protest as a human-interest story focusing on Native people, celebrities, and war veterans. Both outlets addressed broad-based public concerns about global climate change, plus water pollution and land rights, but from different perspectives.[68] Fox News reproduced "the colonial narratives found in a 200-year U.S. history of dispossession and genocide perpetrated against Native Americans on these same Lakota-Dakota-Sioux lands."[69,70] The *New York Times* framed the issue as part of a wider environmental and human rights movement, but the researchers were concerned that dominant voices presented in the stories failed to see what the story was really about—which was the sovereign rights of the Lakota and Dakota people.

The researchers found the articles were framed in the all-too-familiar pattern persistent in the historical coverage of Indigenous peoples; this was a hegemonic portrayal of the white settler colonialist structures of state, military, and legal system exercising and aggressively enforcing their self-proclaimed right to occupied Indigenous lands.

The *New York Times* was a focus of the 2021 NAJA *Spotlight Report*. Half of the 300 stories about Indigenous people published in a five-year period (2014–2021) contained stereotypes. Of the 804 stereotypes found, the most frequently used were about violence or vanishing cultures.[71] The people most affected by the stories were also neglected as sources. Articles written by five Indigenous reporters were more likely to use both Indigenous and non-Indigenous sources and less likely to use stereotypical words or phrases as identified by the NAJA Bingo Card, a scorecard to track how publications portray Indigenous people using stereotypes, tropes, and cliches such as casino, alcohol, poverty, violence, and vanishing culture.

The mainstream media only slightly improved in 2021 from 2020 according to NAJA's *Spotlight Reports*.[72] More than half of the coverage found in the *New York Times*, *The Guardian*, *The Washington Post*, Fox News, and NPR used at least one of NAJA'S Bingo Card terms and more than a quarter used at least two terms. Indigenous people were mainly referred to in historical terms and stories relied heavily on officials and not community members. Conversely, Indigenous authors used more Indigenous sources overall. But a slight improvement is hopeful.

The findings of these framing analyses correspond with prior research on the effectiveness of protest events as a means of garnering media attention. Issues that fit best with a media source's ongoing agenda were more likely to be published; unique events which resulted in protests resulted in more coverage than thematic issues focusing on ongoing problems.[73] The analyses revealed that sovereignty is not a theme that the news media understands.

In sum, the research on coverage of Indigenous people and issues in the news media continues to find that Native people are invisible, anachronistic, in opposition to progress, and not reliable sources on issues that directly affect them.

IN-GROUP BIAS

An understanding of in-group bias provides some insight into why reporters frame stories in ways that support the hegemonic structure of the United States keeping Indigenous people off the news agenda and framing them in inaccurate and stereotypical ways. It also provides a framework to understand how much the agenda-setting function of the news media is steeped in colonial structures. First, in-group bias is a concept underlying social identity theory. It assumes that people think positively, rather than negatively, of themselves and part of self-image is defined in terms of group membership. The implication is that individuals view the groups they "belong to" more positively than the groups they "do not belong to."[74] Thus, in-group bias is defined as the tendency to give a more favorable evaluation or treatment to in-group members than to out-group members.

White people generally constitute the in-group, and Indigenous people, and other people of color, the out-group. This is because of the minority status of Natives within the general U.S. population, and their almost complete absence from mainstream newsroom staffs. For example, only twenty-nine Native journalists were on the staff of print and digital newsrooms (and four on online-only news organizations) in the 2018 American Society of News Editors annual census of minority newsroom staff.[75]

Given that there are so few Indigenous reporters on staff with whom to consult, non-Indigenous reporters and editors are not inclined to personally know Native people or be aware of their issues. Thus, the state of consciousness of the mainstream news media is not a Native one, and the result may be a story, or a series of articles that supports the status quo.

The consequence of this lack of awareness and understanding is that reporters may resort to using historical instead of modern narratives about Indigenous people as reference points for their stories. This bias might occur in all phases of reporting a story from the initial assignment to sourcing, framing, and placement, and then again in the editing process. This may also result in the use of stereotypical phrases by the reporter and/or editors involved.

Due to lack of cross-cultural personal relationships and/or understanding, leading to a reduced comfort level, reporters may be more comfortable consulting with non-Indigenous sources than Indigenous sources. Likewise, reporters might also be more likely to write or produce the story with a negative tone, or to not strive to include context. Editors might place stories differently than if they were not Indigenous focused.

For example, an art story might appear in the "Metro" section. The *Reading Red Report* noted that non-Native issue stories which would generally appear in an entertainment or lifestyle section often invoked more of a hard news approach and were incorrectly printed in the "Metro" section. Additionally, phrases such as "circle the wagons," "wander off the reservation," and "smoke the peace pipe" might be published without consideration of their historical meaning whether in stories about Indigenous people or not.

Even when unintended on a conscious level, stories may be stereotypical; might not cover a broad range of issues; and might not put the story into context. The agenda-setting function of the news media may play a role as to whether the story is assigned and then followed up. Finally, in-group bias may also contribute to the misconception that Indians "get something for nothing and have unique advantages" by being able to operate casinos.

Therefore, it is highly likely that Indigenous people and the issues tribal members, individually and their communities, face may be overlooked—just as it is highly unlikely that reporters or editors understand the importance of sovereignty.

The news media's attraction to covering tribal gaming operations and not sovereignty issues may be the result of the intersection of framing, in-group bias, and agenda setting. Aside from the occasional onslaught of media stories surrounding a specific event and as previously illustrated in this book about environmental issues, tribal gaming operations receive the most coverage by mainstream media outlets. These gaming operations upset the status quo and pose a threat to mainstream economic development and interests. "White responses to tribal casinos are often deeply imbued with racial and colonial discourses, in which people and Nations of color are either supposed to be subordinate to whites or forbidden to have any rights different from those of whites."[76]

Indigenous news organizations that publish for their communities seek to counteract this damaging discourse. This is one of the many reasons that Indigenous news sources are so important.

NOTES

1. Extracted from: Cramer, 2005.
2. Trahant, 2000.
3. "Bush on Native American Issues" (2004–2008).
4. Shear, Knowles, Soden, & Castro, 2015.
5. Rokeach, 1960.
6. Mitchell, Gottfried, & Masta, 2014.
7. Fremlin, 2008.
8. Heider, 2000, p. 81.
9. Bruck, 1989.
10. Hallin, 1986.
11. Hallin, 1987
12. Carragee, 1991.
13. Gitlin, 1980.
14. Kellner, 1990.
15. Heider, 2000.
16. Shah, McLeod, Gotlieb, & Lee, 2009.
17. McCombs & Estrada, 1997.
18. McCombs & Ghanem, 2001.
19. Miller, 2007.
20. Jamieson & Capella, 1998.
21. Patterson, 2016.
22. Paletz, 1998.

23. Linsky, 1998.
24. O'Heffernan, 1991.
25. Spitzer, 1993.
26. Reese, 2001.
27. Entman, 1993.
28. Iyengar, 1991.
29. Gamson, 1992.
30. Gitlin, 1980.
31. Pan & Kosicki, 1993.
32. Price & Tewksbury, 1997.
33. Hallahan, 1999.
34. Miller & Ross, 2004.
35. Pilger, 1988.
36. Loew, 2011.
37. Larson, 2006.
38. Tallent, 2013.
39. Paletz, 1998.
40. Ashley & Olsen, 1998, p. 263.
41. Edelman, 1988, 12–13.
42. Wilkins, 2007, p. 238.
43. Copeland, 1977.
44. Shaughnessy, 1978.
45. Stensland, 1974.
46. Hanson & Rouse, 1987.
47. Hanson & Rouse, 1987.
48. Hall, 1995.
49. Robert Berkofer, *The White Man's Indian*, 1978.
50. Alia, 2004.
51. Mary Weston, *Native Americans in the News,* 1996.
52. Mary Weston, *Native Americans in the News*, 1996.
53. Coward, 1999.
54. Brigg, 2003.
55. Carstarphen & Sanchez, 2006.
56. Heider, 2000.
57. Torres & González, 2011.
58. Leavy & Maloney, 2006.
59. Daniels, 2006.
60. Daniels, 2006.
61. LaPoe et al., 2018, p. 190.
62. Briggs, 2002.
63. Azocar, 2007.
64. Gray, 2016.
65. Martini, 2008.
66. Moore, 2018.
67. Moore, 2018, p. 109.

68. Walker & Walter, 2018.
69. Fenelon, 2014.
70. Grua, 2016.
71. 2021 NAJA Media *Spotlight Report,* https://najanewsroom.com/2021-naja-media-spotlight-report/.
72. 2020 NAJA Media *Spotlight Report,* https://najanewsroom.com/2020-naja-media-spotlight-report/; 2021 NAJA Media *Spotlight Report,* https://najanewsroom.com/2021-naja-media-spotlight-report/.
73. Smith, McCarthy, McPhail, & Augustyn, 2001.
74. Brewer & Pierce, 2005.
75. This data was acquired from the American Society of News Editors Annual Census, 2018 (see: https://www.asne.org/diversity-survey-percent).
76. Klopotek, 2011.

Chapter 5

Indigenous Standpoint Theory and News Coverage

Indigenous Standpoint Theory (IST) is best applied to analyzing media texts in a similar way that research has applied to Indigenous knowledge in educational thinking. "Indigenous Standpoint Theory elevates Indigenous pedagogy by contextualizing the content into meaningful cultural and social perspectives that Indigenous learners and their communities can relate to."[1] By replacing pedagogy with "content" and "learners" with "news media" and "audience," the following framework emerges, which is that IST elevates Indigenous news media by contextualizing the content into meaningful cultural and social perspective with which Indigenous audiences and their communities can relate.

This framework also applies to the outcome of research in the pursuit of increased knowledge and participation in community. "Programs developed and implemented in partnership with Indigenous people and communities result in improved outcomes and participation."[2] It follows that news coverage developed and implemented in partnership with Indigenous people and communities, results in improved knowledge and participation in Indigenous communities. The importance of news media that take an Indigenous standpoint is summed up by Bryan Pollard, former associate director and past president of the Native American Journalists Association and citizen of Cherokee Nation, in the following:

> Indigenous people across North America depend on Native media outlets for essential information about their communities and tribal affairs. These newspapers, newsletters, magazines, radio and television broadcasts as well as online publications are often produced in places that otherwise lack a reliable source of timely, accurate and contextual coverage of what impacts their daily lives. Indigenous media, however, does more than distribute news. It serves

as a community forum that can help reinforce cultural values and languages. Ultimately, it holds the potential to reaffirm an Indigenous community's identity.[3]

When analyzing media texts, Indigenous researchers easily identify tropes that are missed by non-Indigenous researchers. Journalism organizations, such as the Native American Journalists Association, have pushed for diversity in newsrooms to decrease the publication of these harmful tropes. Academic institutions must also acknowledge that the dismissal of non-Indigenous researchers "seeing" their damaging impact perpetuates colonizer knowledge-sharing systems.

IST and other decolonizing research theories are in response to Western traditions that exclude and exploit Indigenous communities from both the process and the outcome of the research. In contrast, research that influences policy and shapes harmful practices that impact Indigenous communities emerge from Western knowledge or forms of inquiry.[4] Although research from Indigenous perspectives and by Indigenous people is often misinterpreted, appropriated, and dismissed in academia, it is those Western spaces that provide its ability to thrive.[5]

> By including an Indigenous-based framework in the research presented in this book, it is the author's fervent hope to persuade journalism critics, journalism educators, and journalists to examine the practice of journalism from a different perspective, and, then, to incorporate that perspective into their journalistic practices, because as Vine Deloria Junior notes "Indians are alive, have certain dreams of their own, and are being overrun by the ignorance and the mistaken, misdirected efforts of those who would help them."[6]

Indigenous scholarship examining the colonial history of social and scientific research originated in the field of education in Australia and elsewhere,[7,8,9,10,11,12,13,14,15,16,17,18,19,20,21,22] and IST was first used in literary work in Australia, but is now being applied to other disciplines such as education,[23] feminist studies,[24] climate change,[25] and more recently health studies.[26] It evolved from feminist standpoint theory, which developed out of women's needs to have a format for research that made sense of and countered the paternalistic-dominated, as well as Western-dominated, discourse in the humanities and social sciences,[27] which maintains the power structure of the academy.[28,29,30,31] Feminist standpoint theory, however, was predominantly based on a white-feminist perspective; it did not incorporate the various experiences of women of color[32] and did not recognize that Indigenous perspectives were grounded in notions of sovereignty.

Rights, citizen status, and sovereignty are core parts of Indigenous researchers' lives and studies, so they are generally how Native academics position their research. Non-Indigenous scholars rarely consider these critical values in their research. Instead, they frame their studies about Indigenous issues in terms of concepts such as postcolonial theory and social justice.[33] It is the failure to consider sovereignty that perpetuates colonial knowledge.[34] It is the failure of non-Indigenous journalists to consider the fundamental importance of sovereignty in their coverage of the federal recognition process that allows perpetuation of incomplete and inaccurate stories about the reason Tribes seek federal recognition.

IST uses the perspective of the researcher to understand the implications of what she or he is "seeing." Indigenous knowledge is a complex system that does not easily fit into Western logic.[35] Any discussion of alleviating disparities within Indigenous communities must include Indigenous knowledge. Unfortunately, Indigenous knowledge seems only used in areas of study that align with stereotypes of Indigenous people as being of the natural or mystical world. Therefore, it is more likely for an interested person to find studies which incorporate Indigenous knowledge in the fields of climate change, conservation, and other environmental issues.[36,37,38,39] Likewise, it is more likely for an interested person to find studies when Indigenous people fall behind socially in areas of education and health.[40,41]

One of the goals of using IST is to acknowledge the research needs and priorities of Indigenous people and to change the balance of power in the academy.[42] The IST that applied in this research utilizes the author's understanding as an Indigenous person, as well as a critic of the news media because of her years of reading, watching, and listening to non-Indigenous news publications stereotyping, denigrating, and blaming Native people for their "standing" in the world.

The first study of the news media using IST examined the difference in mainstream and Indigenous news coverage of the COVID-19 crises in Indian County.[43] It revealed the ways economic inequality and non-Native individuals' misunderstandings of Indigenous gaming operations led to stereotypical news coverage of Indigenous communities during the early months of the COVID-19 pandemic in 2020. This study showed the ways in which mainstream media used "parachute reporting" to create a one-sided view of the pandemic's impacts on Indian Country, particularly when it came to tribal casinos and other industries, which are necessary to fund indispensable tribal functions. IST highlighted the differences in these narratives and differentiated the ways that Indigenous people tell their stories, in contrast to non-Native reporters and their media companies. The study found that non-Indigenous reporters failed to connect gaming operations to the fabric of Indigenous people's lives and mostly focused on loss, which included the lack of, or underfunded resources available, government tensions, and chronic disproportionate struggle. This study found coverage of casinos did include sovereignty, but only in the context that sovereign status afforded Tribes the ability to ignore mandates to shut down their businesses.

When news articles referenced the need of the United States to honor its commitment to Native people, comments from tribal communities were either excluded or buried. Indigenous media focused on health, economic and cultural resilience as well as Tribes' ability to thrive and survive during the initial stages of the pandemic. The textual analysis found casinos were part of the coverage in Indigenous media half as often than non-Indigenous media. Non-Indigenous media focused on the coverage, whereas Indigenous media focused on informing Tribes how the closure of the community, not for-profits, and casinos affected the ability of tribal leaders to support their members.

Indigenous media sources have filled the mainstream media void about issues affecting their communities since the publication of *The Cherokee Phoenix* in 1828.[44,45] This first Indigenous newspaper in the United States provided the Cherokee Nation with information about news and culture, news from other Tribes, and focused on explaining Cherokee realities and values as the Tribe opposed the U.S. government's plans for removal.[46] Contemporary Indigenous journalists continue to work in the tradition of that first newspaper to accurately reflect the communities they report about, to advocate for tribal rights, to preserve traditions, and to help correct mistakes and inaccuracies by mainstream media.[47,48]

The study of news coverage of gaming and COVID-19 revealed that a major theme within Indigenous media was enduring the federal government's disregard for its responsibilities to Tribes. The comparison of the news coverage reveals that there is a significant difference between what Indigenous media know is important to their communities and what non-Indigenous media think is important to Indigenous communities. "Natives writing about Native issues provide an intellectual voice beyond stereotypes."[49] This is a form of colonialism as it "mutes the voices of those who have been marginalized by colonization."[50] IST can be used to assess the construction of "Indians" in the news media.[51]

Mainstream press norms and routines, formed when assimilation was the desired social model, are still not oriented to accurately and objectively cover communities of color.[52] Indigenous media have filled the void left by a lack of mainstream media coverage about issues affecting their communities.[53] Indigenous journalists operate to accurately reflect the communities they report about, to champion coverage of rights, to correct mistakes and misinterpretations by mainstream media, and to preserve traditions.[54,55] The Indigenous cultures of the United States include a complex array of beliefs, values, systems, practices, and traditions that are difficult for outsiders to understand.[56] From a journalistic perspective, IST enables researchers to contextualize the differences between the goals of mainstream journalism and those of Indigenous journalism. In comparison to mainstream journalism, news created by Indigenous journalists provides more meaningful cultural and social perspectives for its audience. This enables Indigenous journalists to address problems at a level[57] that encourages ownership of issues and leads to social responsibility.[58]

NOTES

1. Choy & Woodlock, 2007, p. 42.
2. Choy & Woodlock, 2007, p. 43.
3. From: Pollard, 2020.
4. Kovach, 2009.
5. Kovach, 2009.
6. Extracted from: Deloria, 1988, p. xiii.
7. Tuhiwai-Smith, 1999.
8. Martin, 2008.
9. Rigney, 1997.
10. Steihnauer, 2002.
11. Kahakalau, 2004.
12. Battiste, 1998.
13. Weber-Pillwax, 2001.
14. Porsanger, 2004.
15. Tuhiwia-Smith, 1999.
16. Graham, 2005.
17. Estrada, 2005.
18. Wilson, 2005.
19. Martin, 2008.
20. Nakata, 2007.
21. Wilson, 2008.
22. Tipa et al., 2009.
23. Choy & Woodlock, 2007.
24. Moreton-Robinson, 2013.
25. Srinivasan, 2004.
26. Gilroy et al., 2013.
27. Foley, 2003.
28. Collins, 1997.
29. Harding, 1997.
30. Harstock, 1997.
31. Smith, 1997.
32. Weiss Hanrahan, 2000.
33. Ardill, 2013.
34. Ardill, 2013.
35. Nakata, 2004.
36. Bortona, 2019.

37. Diver, 2017.
38. Eddington, 2017.
39. Green et al., 2010.
40. Choy & Woodlock, 2007.
41. Srinivasan, 2004.
42. Foley, 2013.
43. Azocar et al., 2021.
44. LaPoe & LaPoe, 2017.
45. Murphy, 2010.
46. Murphy, 2010.
47. LaPoe & LaPoe, 2017.
48. Murphy, 2010.
49. LaPoe & LaPoe, 2017, p. 26.
50. Ardill, 2013, p. 318.

51. Nakata's work developing Indigenous Standpoint Theory (IST) assesses colonial knowledge about Indigenous Australians. It exposes the "workings of knowledge and how understandings of Indigenous people is caught up and is implicated in its work." See: Nakata, 2007, p. 12.

52. Wilson, Gutierrez, & Chao, 2013.
53. LaPoe & LaPoe, 2017.
54. LaPoe & LaPoe, 2017.
55. Murphy, 2010.
56. Choy & Woodlock, 2007.
57. Nakata, 2004.
58. Srinivasan, 2004.

Chapter 6

History of News Coverage of Federal Recognition

American Indian nations have always played games, and this gaming was and is an important custom. Traditionally, it served to preserve culture and ceremonies, redistribute wealth, and teach traditional values to community members and children. Skill and luck came together to level the playing field upon which all lived their lives. —Eileen M. Luna-Firebaugh and Mary Jo Tippeconnic Fox[1]

The news media's practices of agenda setting and framing, the problems of in-group bias, and the hegemonic structure of the mainstream media could influence the federal recognition of Tribes. Although there are recent cries of "fake news" and "liberal journalism," the public continues to be influenced by mainstream media. "'Legacy media' are still a primary means by which people orient themselves toward the world beyond their direct experience and, in particular, make sense of their own capacity for individual and collective agency."[2] Policymakers and policy influences are also persuaded by news.[3] They rely on newspapers in print and online as well as radio and television to stay informed on matters.[4]

Scholars who study policy acknowledge the media's role in agenda setting, noting that media attention is episodic, providing high levels of attention to some issues, but ignoring most. Policy studies provide evidence of the role of the media in the policy cycle through "positive feedback (increased levels of coverage) and negative feedback (low levels of coverage, or no coverage) into the system, corresponding with changes in the intensity of policymaking activity."[5]

The agenda-setting function on both national and local news coverage of Indigenous issues tend to result in a surge of reporting on a particular issue, followed by silence. Often labeled parachute reporting, journalists are sent to a location to cover breaking news, only to leave when the next story hits.

Given that silence is the norm for coverage of Indian Country, it can be especially detrimental because it is often the only story the general public will see or hear about Indigenous people for long stretches of time. Recent examples are the Hantavirus outbreak on the Navajo Reservation in 1993; the school shooting on the Red Lake Indian Reservation in 2005; the Dakota Access Pipeline (DAPL) protests in 2017, the devastating consequences of COVID-19 due to underfunding, and mascots used by sports teams.[6] The time between each of these events has generally been about a decade, and is event or action centered and focuses on conflict.[7] The news media isolate Indigenous issues by focusing on one event with a distinct beginning and ending, and rarely with context and follow-up. These stories adhere to the most basic form of agenda setting: an event centered on a specific group of people in conflict. The stories produced from these events are then framed episodically and without context. The most salient part of the story is missing. Why did it happen?

FRAMING OF FEDERAL RECOGNITION AND CASINOS

In the past few decades, many Tribes have faced negative media attention because of their use of gaming as a means of tribal self-reliance.[8,9] The ability for federally recognized Tribes to operate gaming establishments is in opposition to the colonial status quo. The agenda-setting function of the news media has put tribal casino operations at the top of the news, and they have become the most reported story related to Indian Country. The media are so focused on gaming in Indian Country that is has become the core of stories about Tribes, even when only tangentially related to gaming. Sovereignty issues and rights inherent in the operation of casinos are arguably more important to Tribes than any other topic. This is because without sovereignty, functioning as an Indigenous Nation is extremely difficult. Therefore, Tribes will spend decades plodding through the daunting process of federal acknowledgment. However, mainstream journalists do not understand tribal sovereignty as a legal principle; their tendency to combine it with programs such as Affirmative Action can have adverse consequences for Tribes.[10]

The narrative of gaming entered the federal recognition process in the 1980s with the expansion of tribal bingo operations and the growth of casino-style gaming. Revenue-raising efforts through gaming began in the 1970s, when several Tribes began offering high-stakes bingo on their reservations or tribal lands. Tribes hoped to improve the standard of living for their members by means of the jobs created through gaming, along with the revenue it brought in from the business. In other words, gaming presented a new economic opportunity for Tribes as these bingo halls were very successful.[11]

Once bingo challenged the big-money power brokers who traditionally controlled gaming operations, the direction of news reporting on Indian issues changed. In the 1960s and 1970s, stories of Native people coalesced around the occupation of Alcatraz by young activists in the San Francisco Bay Area in California.[12] On the heels of the *Kerner Report* in 1988,[13] and the beginning of the so-called Golden Age of diversity in news media hiring and coverage,[14] reporting of the Alcatraz occupation and other Indigenous issues became more nuanced. But those stories, such as the use of Indian representations for sports teams, did not significantly challenge the economic interests of the status quo. Then, everything changed in the mid-1980s when the Cabazon Band of Mission Indians opened a high-stakes bingo parlor near Palm Springs in California. Until Indians got good at providing entertainment for revenue, it wasn't a problem. But once Tribes figured out how beneficial it could be to supporting tribal infrastructure, it was challenged.

The State of California shut the operation down as a violation of its gambling laws in 1986. But in 1987, the U.S. Supreme Court ended California's shutdown confirming that in Indian Country states can only exercise those powers given to them by Congress, and Congress never gave the States the power to regulate tribal gaming.[15] *California v. Cabazon Band of Mission Indians* in 1987[16] held that state governments do not have the authority to regulate gaming activities on Indian reservations.[17] The *Cabazon Band*, (along with the *Morongo Band of Mission Indians* in California) operated profitable bingo halls on their reservations. Prior to the Indian Gaming Regulatory Act (IGRA) of 1988, it was a misdemeanor to offer bingo except for a charity and for a maximum pot of $250.[18] IGRA provided a statutory basis for the gaming industry and preserved tribal rights to operate casino-style facilities.[19] The Supreme Court's decision meant that States could not enforce their gaming regulations on Indian reservations. Gaming brought the much-needed revenue to Native Nations, which helped tribal governments provide employment, health, housing, and education services to tribal members. In 2019, Indian gaming was a $34.6 billion business with more than 246 tribal governments operating 522 gaming facilities in 29 states.[20] Gaming revenue declined for the first time in 2020 because of the COVID-19 pandemic.[21] Even with that $27.8 billion decrease, tribal leaders were able to lead the way in developing innovative safety protocols, sharing community resources, and creating new standards. "Tribal gaming has shown resilience and commitment and continues to develop new roads to economic stability," NIGA Vice Chair Jeannie Hovland concluded in the 2020 NIGA, Gaming Revenue Reports.[22]

IGRA created the National Indian Gaming Commission (NIGC) to support tribal self-sufficiency and the integrity of Indian gaming. The NIGC has four initiatives to support its mission. These are: (1) To protect against anything that amounts to gamesmanship on the backs of tribes; (2) To stay ahead of the

Technology Curve; (3) Rural outreach; and (4) To maintain a strong workforce within NIGC and with its tribal regulatory partners. However, there are complaints that IGRA (the Act) actually limits the power of Tribes because they have the inherent right to engage in gaming on their reservations. The Act gave state governments some control over gaming enterprises.[23] For example, consequent to the IGRA, Utah does not allow any form of gaming, so the Tribes in Utah cannot engage in Class II or Class III gaming.[24]

Because of a media-constructed connection of gaming with Indians, a common misconception is that all Tribes are making enormous amounts of money for their members. In fact, fewer than half of all federally recognized Tribes have gaming operations, many of these businesses are not that lucrative because they are not near places with large populations of non-Indians. It is important to remember that most reservation lands are in rural areas,[25] and not readily accessible to those seeking to gamble.

Despite this reality, potential gaming revenue is brought into question when a Tribe decides to pursue federal recognition and whether Upper Mattaponi Indian Tribe have to make concessions to receive it. For example, the Upper Mattaponi Tribe[26] in Virginia first petitioned for federal recognition in 1974. In 2006, Senator John McCain asked at a Committee on Indian Affairs hearing[27] whether the Tribe would consider opening a casino if it received recognition. Upper Mattaponi Chief Kenneth Adams[28] responded "no," that the Upper Mattaponi are Baptist and had no plans to pursue gaming as the Baptist Christian sect strongly disapproves of any form of gaming.[29] But federal recognition should not be contingent on a tribe's gaming interests.

The Upper Mattaponi, along with five additional Tribes in Virginia, received recognition through an act of Congress in early 2018. However, when the Thomasina E. Jordan Indian Tribes of Virginia Federal Recognition Act of 2017 passed, it effectively forever prohibited those six Tribes from conducting gaming activities.

This raises a national societal problem in terms of the dominant culture's capacity to determine how Indigenous issues are viewed by the nation as a whole. This conflating of the association of gaming with federal acknowledgment is problematic for Tribes seeking federal recognition.[30] When the news media adds the gaming narrative to their coverage of Tribes, whether or not that Tribe has expressed interest in pursuing gaming operations, it can skew political and public opinion against that recognition.

This is the first analysis of how the news media cover federal recognition. It uses content analysis as an exploratory approach to examining the coverage in order to understand whether Tribes seeking federal recognition only make the news when that pursuit puts them in conflict with the status quo. It uses Moore's technique as described in journalism, politics, and the Dakota Access Pipeline, in which she identified some of the frames by searching for specific language such as phrases or slogans that appeared in the sample of articles.[31]

Using this framework, this analysis of news media coverage of federal recognition seeks to answer a number of questions. How often do stories about federal recognition actually occur? To what extent do the news media conflate gaming and federal recognition? Do the journalistic norms of framing and agenda setting, and the hegemonic structure, which allows for in-group bias, prioritize gaming over the pursuit of sovereignty in news coverage? How does the news coverage in Indigenous news organizations differ?

NOTES

1. Luna-Firebaugh & Fox, 2010, p. 75.
2. Hacket et al., 2017.
3. Fawzi, 2018.
4. Mesce, 2018.
5. Russel, Dwidar, & Jones, 2016.
6. The coverage of mascots has been ongoing. It started in the late 1980s and peaked around 2007.
7. Schudson, 2011..
8. McCulloch & Wilkins, 1995.
9. Pevar, 2002.
10. Lowe & Mella, 2005.
11. Pevar, 2004.
12. Westin, 1996.
13. Kerner Commission, National Advisory Commission on Civil Disorders (1988). *Kerner Report*, 1968.
14. I suggest the "Golden Age of diversity" began when mainstream media organizations and nonprofit organizations started funding diversity programs and supporting organizations that supported ethnic minority journalists such as the Asian American Journalists Association, the National Association of Black Journalists, the Native American Journalists Association and the National Association of Hispanic Journalists. It ended when Unity, Journalists of Color disbanded in 2018.
15. Rossum, 2011.
16. In *California v. Cabazon Band of Mission Indians*, 480 U.S. 202 (1987) The Court held that "the State's interest in preventing the infiltration of the tribal bingo enterprises by organized crime does not justify state regulation of the tribal bingo enterprises in light of the compelling federal and tribal interests supporting them. State regulation would impermissibly infringe on tribal government[.]"
17. Finkelman & Garrison, 2009.
18. Pevar, 2004.
19. Finkelman & Garrison, 2009.
20. See: National Indian Gaming Commission, Gaming Revenue Reports, 2019.
21. See: National Indian Gaming Commission, Gaming Revenue Reports, 2020.

22. See National Indian Gaming Commission, Gaming Revenue Reports, 2020.
23. Pevar, 2004.
24. Pevar, 2004.
25. See the Rural Information Hub (www.ruralhealthinfo.org/topics/rural-tribal-health).
26. Interview with Chief Kenneth Adams.
27. Author's own notes from the Thomasina Jordan Indian Tribes of Virginia Federal Recognition Act and the Grand River Band of Ottawa Indians of Michigan Referral Act Hearing before the Committee on Indian Affairs United States s. 437 and s. 480 June 21, 2006, Washington, DC https://www.gpo.gov/fdsys/pkg/CHRG-109shrg28348/html/CHRG-109shrg28348.htm.
28. Author's own notes.
29. Louishomme, 2003.
30. Cramer, 2005.
31. Moore, 2018.

Chapter 7

Forty Years of News Coverage of Federal Recognition

To understand the history of the news media's coverage of federal recognition, it's important to track that coverage over time and see what has changed and what has remained static. Examining both mainstream media and Indigenous media and the Western and Indigenous theoretical perspectives provides answers to the questions posed at the end of the previous chapter.

Hegemonic theory working in conjunction with agenda-setting theory would predict that, because of the racial structure of most newsrooms, stories about federal recognition are not on the agenda and, therefore, would be scarce. Moreover, because federal recognition is not generally event centered, it is not considered a newsworthy "minority" story. Meanwhile, it is possible that stereotypical words and phrases will be published because journalists are not sensitive to them, and editors will miss them. For published stories, agenda-setting theory would predict that news about Tribes seeking federal recognition would support government positions on whether a Tribe should be recognized or not by the conflation of federal recognition and Indian gaming operations, which confuses a real understanding of the need for federal recognition by Tribes. Additionally, framing theory would predict that more stories would include a casino frame than a tribal sovereignty frame.

Undertaking the research for this book sought to elucidate whether and how news coverage influences decision-making bodies through the lens of hegemonic theory. The majority of Congress is white and male. Federal recognition of Tribes would grant the recipient Tribes a greater measure of power, which is antithetical to those white supremacist values such as upheld by many national, as well as state, political leaders.

Since agenda-setting theory would predict that few stories would be published or produced about Tribes and federal recognition is important to examine the largest number of relevant articles possible. Therefore, the available universe of stories included in academic databases was used to gather print, broadcast (radio and television), and online stories. The goal is to answer some broad questions about coverage of federal recognition and how or whether it has changed over time. But also of interest is the news coverage of the Virginia Tribes that were recently recognized, which up to the recent federal recognition had only state-recognized Tribes. As noted earlier, the Pamunkey Tribe of Virginia received recognition through the BIA Federal Acknowledgment Process in 2015. The Chickahominy, the Chickahominy Indian Tribe-Eastern Division, the Upper Mattaponi, the Rappahannock, the Monacan, and the Nansemond Tribe received recognition through a legislative act, the Thomasina E. Jordan Indian Tribes of Virginia Federal Recognition Act in 2018.

NEWS COVERAGE OF FEDERAL RECOGNITION OF TRIBES

The following are the questions posed for the research foundational to the creation of this book: How many mainstream print/online stories and how many mainstream radio or television broadcast stories were published about federal recognition during the time indexed by the databases up to February 2018? Are stereotypical phrases and words common in stories about federal recognition? Based on agenda setting and framing theory, it's expected the majority of mainstream stories will be framed as "casino" stories and not "tribal sovereignty" stories.

Congressional hearing testimony is also expected to follow a similar pattern of the news media and focus on casinos and not tribal sovereignty.

Proquest Global Newstream[1] was searched to gather a sample of newspaper and magazine articles and news blogs published in English as far back as indexed by the database. Proquest provides full-text access to more than 2,500 news sources, including newspapers, magazines, newswires, news journals, television and radio transcripts, blogs, podcasts, and digital-only websites. The following key newspapers and online sites are indexed along with regional newspapers, including more than eighty Gannett-owned regional and local titles:

- The *New York Times* (backfile from 1977 forward)
- *The Wall Street Journal* (from 1984 forward)
- *The Washington Post* (from 1987 forward)
- *Los Angeles Times* (from 1985 forward)
- *Chicago Tribune* (from 1985 forward)

- *Boston Globe* (from 1997 forward)
- *Newsday* (from 1995 forward)
- *The Wall Street Journal* (online)
- *ProPublica*
- *Huffington Post*
- *CNN Newswires*

A search of English-language articles published in U.S. news sources, but excluding Indigenous publications, were collected using the search terms "federal recognition" or "federal acknowledgement" and "American Indian(s)" or "Native American(s)" from any date to February 28, 2018. This end date was chosen to capture all stories published one month after the passage of the Jordan Act on January 29, 2018. Source types included blogs, podcasts/websites; magazines; newspapers; and wire feeds. Document types included articles; blogs; commentary; editorials; features; front page/cover stories; news; websites/webcasts.

Broadcast Sample

Lexis Nexis transcripts were used to examine broadcast coverage of federal recognition from the oldest date indexed up to February 28, 2018. Lexis Nexis indexes thirty U.S. broadcast newscasts including the following key mainstream sites: (See Appendix A for a complete list of broadcast sources indexed by Lexis Nexis.)

- ABC News
- CBS News
- NBC News
- NPR
- CNN
- PBS NewsHour
- C-SPAN

Print/Online Stories

The search of print and online stories resulted in 3,859 articles: 3,170 newspaper articles, 631 wire feeds, 52 blogs and websites, and 6 magazine articles between August 16, 1981 and February 25, 2018. Online sources were the *New York Times*-online (54 stories), *Politico* (6 stories), *The Washington Post*-online (5 stories), the *Hartford* Courant-online (3 stories), *Huffington Post* (3 stories), the *Los Angeles Times*-online (2 stories), the *Baltimore Sun*-online (1 story), and the *Hamilton Spectator* (1 story).

Wire feed stories were from *McClatchy Tribune Business News* (300), *Knight Ridder Tribune Business News* (118 stories), Gannett News Service (78 stories), *TCA Regional News* (76 stories), AP English Language News (13 stories), Knight Ridder Tribune News Service (11 stories), Dow Jones Institutional News (9 stories), U.S Newswire (8 stories), McClatchy Tribune News Service (6 stories), AP Worldstream (5 stories), Newhouse News Service (3 stories), UPI Newstrack and TCA New Service (1 story).

Only 3,859[2] articles were published in print/online news sources in more than four decades. An average of eighty-six articles per year were published in 101 indexed news sources from across the country in forty-five years. Most articles were news stories (93.5 percent) and fewer than 7 percent were editorials.

Only six magazine articles were published during the timeframe even though ProQuest indexes forty-two English-language magazines, twenty-three from the United States (see Appendix B for a complete list of magazines indexed by ProQuest). Three were from the *New York Times Magazine*, one from the *Weekly Standard*, one from *New Mexico Business Journal*, and one from *Texas Monthly*. The *New Mexico Business Journal* article was the oldest published in 1996, and the *New York Times Magazine* published the latest story in 2017.

The following stereotypical phrases and words commonly associated with Native Americans were searched for within the articles to see how commonly they are used in reporting: "wandering off the reservation," "circle the wagons," "smoke the peace pipe," "real Indian," "don't look Indian," "playing Indian," "bury the hatchet," "happy hunting ground," and "wampum." Only one article used "peace pipe" in a stereotypical way. The editorial, published in the *San Francisco Chronicle* in 2001,[3] not only used "peace pipe," but also "papoose." Another editorial reads "this is all about big wampum. If these tribal remnants can win federal recognition, they get to open casinos."[4] Both of these appeared in newspapers.

Because of the large number of articles found, a visual representation using a word cloud would be helpful to see what the most common words in the stories were and to get a sense of what terms might indicate sovereignty or casino that were not obvious. The word cloud represents all the words that appeared within the articles. The bigger and bolder a word appears, the more often it appeared in the collection of stories.[5] (See figure 7.1)

The image shows that casinos and gambling and gaming are often used words, as is "land." Of note in the image are the words "Hartford" and "Connecticut." The Mashantucket Pequot Tribe, located in southeastern Connecticut, which owns and operates Foxwoods Resort Casino, is one of the largest and most successful casinos among North American Native and

Figure 7.1 Word Cloud from the 3,859 Articles. Word cloud created on Flourish by Simon Rogers, *Google News Lab*

non-Native gaming operations. Foxwoods is often used as a reference point by the news media for Tribes seeking federal recognition because of its success.

The majority of the articles about federal recognition also contained references to gaming operations. Almost 70 percent of stories from all sources contained one of the following terms: casino(s), gaming, games, gambling, or bingo, and most of the stories from every type of source referenced gaming. Most articles were news stories (95.7 percent) and fewer than 6 percent were editorials.

As expected, fewer articles contained tribal sovereignty frames. Just over a quarter of all articles (26.7 percent) included either the term sovereignty or sovereign. The sovereignty search terms were added to the gaming search terms to further understand the association between the two frames within the articles. Most gaming stories did not reference sovereignty (95 percent), but the combined framing of gaming and sovereignty was also the most varied by source. The majority of the stories (69 percent) that included sovereignty also included referenced gaming.

All but one of the six magazine stories included both gaming and sovereignty. Newspapers were the least likely to include both frames, only 2.8 percent or 88 of the stories did. About one-third of the fifty-two blog and website articles included both frames (17 stories).

A separate search examined the universe of television and radio broadcast stories. Only twenty-two news programs were aired on any of the thirty stations indexed through February 28, 2018, specifically focused on Native Americans. An additional 161 mentioned Indigenous people within the context of other news. Although difficult to analyze based on the low number, the absence of news and its limited scope is also telling. The oldest broadcast aired on August 13, 1993 and the newest on April 30, 2016. National Public Radio aired the majority of the stories from six of its sources: All Things Considered (5); Talk of the Nation (4); Morning Edition (2); News and Notes (1); Day to Day (1) and Tavis Smiley (1). CNN aired two stories and the following programs/stations aired one each: C-SPAN, *60 Minutes*, KFVE *Evening News at 6:30* (Honolulu, HI); Fox Business News (John Stossel). In twenty-three years, fewer than one story per year aired on broadcast television about federal recognition. (See Appendix E for a complete list of the mainstream broadcast stories that include references to federal recognition.)

Only two stories aired any of the common stereotypical words. "A Nation of Freeloaders" aired on Stossel's Fox program in 2012 and it also contained the phrase "circle the wagons." The weekly talk show program appeared on Fox Business Network show and aired from 2009 to 2016. "Your Land is My Land" aired on the ABC program *20/20* and was the first program indexed in the search in 1993. One of the guests said, "My ancestors took their land. They got something in return. They got their food, their blankets, their clothing, their hatchet, their whatever."

In one story, even the transcribers are subject to stereotyping when doing their job, or if it was done electronically, it was not corrected. In the CNN news story titled *Invisible People, Identity Crises*, then Assistant Secretary Ada Deer's name was transcribed as "Eat A Deer."[6] Secretary Deer is a citizen of the Menominee Tribe.

A second word cloud was created to examine the most prevalent words in the transcripts of broadcast news stories. To reduce the chance of the image finding words used in the transcript to denote audience actions or directions such as "applause" "voice over" and "cut to commercial," they were deleted prior to creating the image. (See figure 7.2.) The most prevalent words did not follow the same pattern as that of print/online stories.

However, nineteen of the stories (86 percent) included dialogue about gaming operations, even though only four were specifically about casinos. Twelve stories contained sovereign or sovereignty and ten of those stories included the term sovereign or sovereignty, two in the headline. It was assumed that congressional hearing testimony would follow a similar pattern of the news media and focus on casinos and not tribal sovereignty given that policymakers use the media as a source of policy information. A word cloud was also created from these documents to examine the most prevalent words found within the 311 congressional testimony hearings transcriptions that occurred between December 1972 and February 2018 in *Congressional*

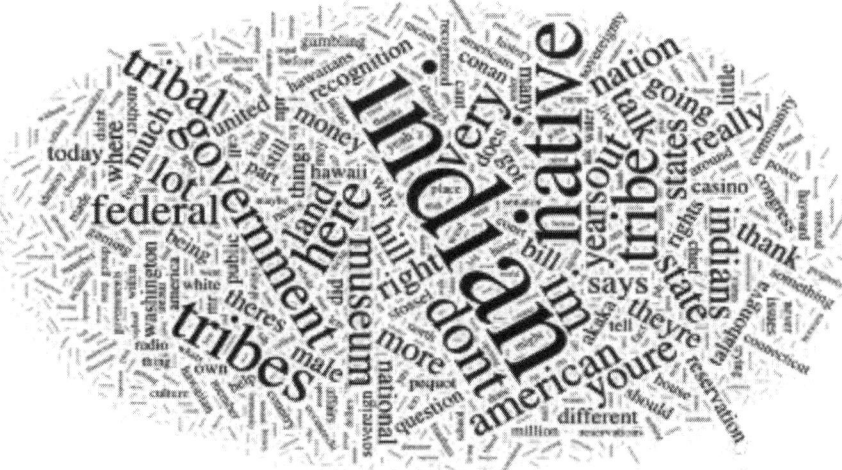

Figure 7.2 Word Cloud of Broadcast News Stories. Word cloud created on Flourish by Simon Rogers, *Google News Lab*

Figure 7.3 Word Cloud of Congressional Testimony. Word cloud created on Flourish by Simon Rogers, *Google News Lab*

Quarterly—"Roll Call on LexisNexis." The first hearing in this time period was September 10, 1993 and the last October 25, 2017. (See figure 7.3.)

The word cloud did not indicate that either gaming or sovereignty discussions were prevalent in the congressional hearings. However, 119 (38.3

percent) of the transcripts included references to gaming, and almost half (155) referenced sovereignty (49.9 percent). Just over a quarter included discussions about both gaming and sovereignty (77).

Mainstream Media Findings

The mainstream media findings on the coverage of federal recognition of Native American Tribes were analyzed in the research study through the theoretical lenses of agenda setting, framing, and hegemony. Interpreting the results through IST shows how pernicious the colonial values on which the United States was founded perpetuate themselves through the mainstream media.

Non-Indigenous reporters, and therefore their readers, misunderstand tribal sovereignty and do not understand how it informs public debate over federal recognition.[7] As predicted, the news media perpetuated ignorance and stereotypes about the sovereignty of Native Tribes by keeping Tribes' pursuits of recognition off the news agenda, and by overplaying gaming frames and underplaying sovereignty frames. In this way, they replace the old ignoble savage stereotype that threatened violence, with the new "casino Indian" stereotype that reflects the fear of the economic and political threat that Native people pose.[8]

Because few Indigenous journalists work in mainstream media to serve as a check to the reporting process, mostly undertaken by white journalists educated in a system that ignores Native history, the white supremacist system has been able to perpetuate its hegemony in the media and make Indian people invisible. According to the News Leaders Association, in 2015 (the last year the organization completed an annual census of newsroom diversity), less than one-half of one percent of journalists working in mainstream news organization were Native. A few mainstream news organizations have introduced Indigenous affairs desk in the last few years, including *High Country News* in Paonia, Colorado and the *Texas Observer* in Austin, Texas. The *Seattle Times* and the *Arizona Republic* and Associated Press do have reporters assigned to specifically cover Native American issues, but these represent a small fraction of the news organization around the country. *Indian Country Today's* weekly broadcast available on Arizona PBS is one of the few broadcast organizations with an Indigenous collaboration. First Nations Experience (FNX), a national broadcast television network devoted to Indigenous content worldwide is available to PBS affiliates, community and tribal stations, and cable television providers. In 2020, a collaboration between the Native American Journalists Association and Report for America began to provide support for nineteen Indigenous journalists to cover Indigenous affairs and other beats. Enough efforts, however, aren't underway.

Native Americans suffer from chronic misrepresentation and erasure by an established press, which continually fails to acknowledge the Indigenous timeline. This crisis—a word not used enough to describe Native Americans' efforts against invisibility—is stoked by the stark absence of Indigenous journalists in newsrooms and further complicated by an Indigenous media largely owned by tribal governments and entities.[9]

During the past forty-five years, Americans were exposed to fewer than 4,000 stories about Native Americans and federal recognition in mainstream media, and how many of them read, watched, or listened to them is not clear. However, those who did read, watch, and/or listen received the message from the mainstream media that casinos are more important to Native people than sovereignty. More stories were produced or published about gaming operations, even when Tribes had not proposed them, than about the reason Tribes seek federal recognition in the first place, which is so they can govern themselves and have the power to retain their cultures. Excerpts from some of these articles show how these patterns have persisted.

In "Abenakis' Chief Pursues Cause Through Conflict,"[10] the *New York Times* reported that Homer St. John, Chief of the Abenaki in Quebec, Canada, and New England sought federal recognition for education, health, and economic reasons as well as for hunting and fishing rights. Although Chief St. John is never quoted as interested in establishing a gaming operation, the reporter wrote the following: Recognition "allows a tribe to establish unregulated gaming operations like bingo parlors."

Five years later, in 1993, the *New York Times* published the story "3 Indian Tribes Stir Casino Fears."[11] That the Tribes had no interest in opening a casino isn't reported until six paragraphs into the story:

> While Nanticoke leaders deny any interest in a casino, and the other two groups say casino gambling is not their main motivation, the actions of all three have aroused deep concern among officials about the impact on the state's casino gambling industry. And former President Trump, who owns three Atlantic City casinos, has responded to the Ramapough initiatives by filing a lawsuit against the Bureau of Indian Affairs seeking to declare the 1988 law unconstitutional.

The *New York Times* story quotes an anthropologist to dispute the ancestral claims of the Tribes, stating its members had intermarried to the point that they were no longer Indian. As described earlier in this book, this is a common tactic that the U.S. government used to get rid of Native people and it forced Tribes to enact anti-miscegenation laws in order to maintain their status as a Tribe.

In a 1974 book, *The Ramapough Mountain People*, Dr. David S. Cohen concluded that there is no historical evidence for early Indian ancestry for the Ramapough people. Instead, wrote Dr. Cohen, then an assistant professor of history at Rutgers University in Newark, the group is descended from free blacks who were culturally Dutch and who tended to marry among themselves. "And in the 19th and 20th centuries," he wrote, "Caucasians and some Indians married into the group."[12] Sovereignty is never reported on.

Almost twenty years later, the *Santa Rosa Press Democrat*, a newspaper serving an area two hours north of San Francisco, California used this lead in a story about the Lytton Band of Pomo Indians purchasing land to build homes and a cultural center. "Bill McCormick has watched his neighbors sell their property one by one to an American Indian Tribe that has steadily acquired land next to Windsor's western boundary."[13] And then it introduces casinos: "Officials and nearby residents also fear the tribe may build a casino, despite its insistence that there are no such plans."

Although many of the broadcast stories went into depth about Tribes that were seeking federal recognition, many of them also relied on the same hegemonic relationship with the United States that the print stories did. (See Appendix D for a complete list of broadcast stories that included references to federal recognition.) Using the lens of IST, some examples from different news outlets over time illustrate the lack of understanding the mainstream broadcast news media has about the reason Tribes seek acknowledgment. They each emphasize money over sovereignty.

- A story titled "Nativeness" on NPR: The Occaneechi Indians of North Carolina want state recognition as a tribe. At stake—power and money;[14]
- An NPR story about the Schaghticoke Tribe's pursuit of federal recognition: "Each year, the federal government recognizes one or two new Indian tribes. It's a prize designation; 200 groups are standing in line. That's partly because recognition means the prospect of millions, even billions of dollars in gambling revenues";[15]
- A Fox Business News story with the title of "A Nation of Freeloaders?" Some American Indians are rich. But others stayed poor, feeding off government. Socialists like you have convinced them to do that";[16]
- Hugh Downs and Barbara Walters started a *20/20* segment with the title: "Your Land is My Land": "Connecticut homeowners are shocked and frustrated defendants in a land claim lawsuit filed by a controversial group of Indians who want a big chunk of land and money and the right to open a big-bucks casino."[17]
- Aaron Brown began a CNN *Newsnight* segment in 2002 with this: "We'll look at the high-stakes game of turning obscure Native American tribes into big-time casino owners through the eyes of a tribe that once had just a log

cabin and $23 to its name. So, who would really make the money if they got their wish?"[18]

One story was more egregious in its use of stereotypes. "Wampum Wonderland: Legitimacy of Casinos Run by Indians" was the headline for a story aired by *60 Minutes* in 2000. Steve Croft's introduction is replete with stereotypical language. The entire introduction is included here as it reveals how even one of the most influential and venerated news organizations fails to understand the connection between sovereignty and casinos.

> It rises out of the back woods of Connecticut like some kind of Wampum Wonderland, Las Vegas with an Indian motif. In fact, if Bugsy Siegal had gone into business with Sitting Bull, their casino might have looked a lot like Foxwoods. Every hour on the hour, the rainmaker statue shoots his laser arrow into the heavens. And every hour on the hour, an indoor storm follows just as certainly as three of a kind beats two pair. Welcome to the land of the not exactly extinct Pequots, and to the largest, most successful casino in the Western Hemisphere, conveniently located on sovereign tribal territory in the heart of the Northeast corridor within a three-hour drive for 22 million Americans. (Kroft, 2000)

It is doubtful at the time that there were many Native people working for CBS who might have seen the story before it aired and pointed out all of the stereotypes and inaccuracies. In fact, it wasn't until 1989 that Hattie Kauffman (Nez Perce) became the first Native journalist who reported a story for a national broadcast and there has only been one other since in 2005.[19]

The next step in the research was to take a closer look and examine the news coverage of the Virginia Tribes that recently received federal recognition.

NOTES

1. LexisNexis was not available at the initial data collection phase of this research. Therefore, it was only used for the broadcast search when it became available.

2. Because Proquest Global Newstream updates the sources it indexes daily, the results from this search will be different from those performed on future dates. The original search was saved to maintain the integrity of the data.

3. Saunders, 2001.

4. Condon, 2004.

5. Simon Rogers at the Google News Lab in San Francisco was given the articles and transcripts and generated the word clouds through Flourish.

6. Frazier, 1991.

7. Lowe & Mella, 2005.

8. (As cited in the previous sentence, Lacroix [who published an article headlined *High Stakes Stereotypes: The Emergence of the "Casino Indian"* in the *Howard Journal of Communication*] defines the "casino Indian" stereotype as one that resurrects and resuscitates some of the oldest and most deeply embedded significations of Native Americans and of Native America.) Lacroix, 2011, p. 3.

9. Monet, 2019.

10. Johnson, 1988.

11. Romano, *New York Times*, 1993.

12. Romano, 1993.

13. Mason, 2011.

14. Hartman, Wertheimer, & Adams, 1998.

15. Lyden & Ydstie, 2002.

16. Stossel, J., "A Nation of Freeloaders?" Fox Business Network, July 5, 2012.

17. Downs & Walters, 1993.

18. Brown, A. CNN, *Newsnight*, December 16, 2002.

19. Although Hattie Kauffmann, Nez Perce, was a senior correspondent for *CBS News This Morning*, she may not have been consulted about the story.

Chapter 8

Coverage of the Federal Recognition of Virginia Tribes

On January 29, 2018, six state-recognized Virginia Tribes were federally recognized by an Act of the U.S. Congress, the Thomasina E. Jordan Indian Tribes of Virginia Federal Recognition Act. The Chickahominy, the Eastern Chickahominy, the Upper Mattaponi, the Rappahannock, the Monacan, and the Nansemond Tribes were not able to produce the requisite records for the BIA's Federal Acknowledgement Process (FAP)[1] because of laws meant to keep white supremacy intact. Prior to that, the only federally recognized Tribe in Virginia was the Pamunkey Tribe, which was acknowledged in 2015 through the FAP. However, it had sought recognition in the past in coalition with the other six recently recognized Tribes.

A BRIEF HISTORY OF THE VIRGINIA TRIBES

When Captain John Smith settled at Jamestown in 1607, he met with the ancestors of the Virginia Tribes. He most likely encountered many different Indigenous people who populated the tidewaters when exploring the area—many of which were part of the Powhatan Confederacy at the time. Even though the history of these Tribes spans centuries, it took decades for the Nations to be recognized as Tribes once they started the process.

The first contact between the Indigenous people of the tidewater area (now known as Virginia) and Europeans occurred around 1570. Estimates of the region's Native population prior to European contact extend upward of 100,000.[2] At the beginning of the eighteenth century, the 104 English settlers that had arrived at Jamestown in April 1607 had grown to more than 60,000 English people.[3] (Figure 8.1 shows the Powhatan area in 1607.)

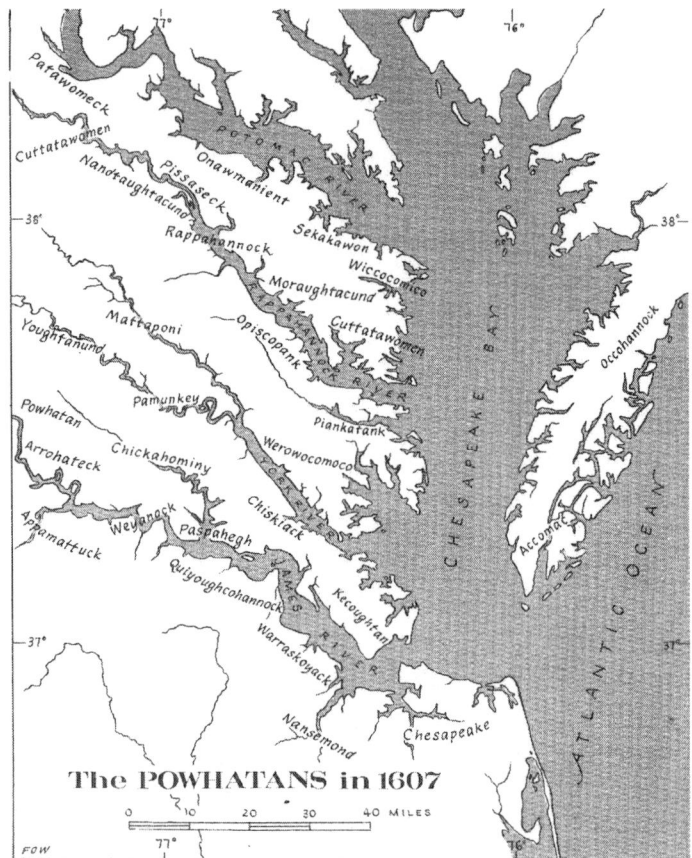

Figure 8.1 Wahunsenacawh Confederacy in 1607. Rountree, Helen C. 1989. The Powhatan Indians of Virginia: Their Traditional Culture. Norman: University of Oklahoma Press "The Powhatans in 1607. Base map after Bathymetry of the Chesapeake Bay (Virginia Institute of Marine Science, 1977)."

Myths abound of Indians based on European accounts of encounters with Chief Wahunsenacawh (Powhatan) and his daughter Matoaka (Pocahontas). The Tribes examined in this research were part of the Wahunsenacawh Confederacy (although the Monocan Tribe was not).[4] They are estimated to have totaled between 10,000 and 15,000 people from 32 Tribes and covering more than 40,000 square miles at the time the English arrived in 1607.[5]

The Pamunkey Reservation in King William County, Virginia—dating back to 1646—is the oldest reservation in the United States. The tribe's 1,200-acre reservation is located on the Pamunkey River. Pamunkey means "Place of the Sweat."

Anthropologist Helen Rountree's examination of Virginia's Tribes provides the most thorough historical accounts of four centuries of their survival, but much of the twentieth-century history of Tribes is scarce most likely because it is estimated that their numbers had been reduced to fewer than 200 by 1790.[6] However, that estimate might have been a convenient number for settlers needing to rid the land of Indians. Although the tribe's populations were decimated by war and disease, they were never removed; they have survived countless campaigns to destroy them, and still they maintain strong ties to the land that they have always lived on. However, because of near annihilation, much of the oral history was lost. Rountree acknowledges that the history of Powhatan culture is therefore seen primarily "through the eyes of people who are removed from us in time and who usually dealt with Indian people for reasons other than pure observation."[7] Federal recognition provides resources that can help Tribes recover cultural loss as well as to preserve culture for future generations.

NEWS COVERAGE OF THE PAMUNKEY TRIBE

Although the Commonwealth of Virginia had recognized the Tribe since the 1700s, it took 400 years of resistance, struggle, and adaptation for the Pamunkey to finally receive federal recognition in 2015. The Tribe began the process in 1980 and collected more than 22,000 pages of history and ancestry to prove its continual existence through the FAP. In its acknowledgment of the Tribe, the U.S. Department of Interior stated, "The Pamunkey Indian Tribe has occupied a land base in southeastern King William County, Virginia—shown on a 1770 map as 'Indian Town'—since the Colonial Era in the 1600s."[8]

The news coverage of the Pamunkey Tribe's pursuit of federal recognition was examined separately from the totality of the stories gathered. The February 28, 2018, cut-off date was kept even though the Tribe received recognition in 2015 because of the six additional Tribes seeking recognition received it in 2018. It was correctly assumed that the Pamunkey's successful bid for recognition would be referenced in the stories of those six Tribes. An analysis of the news coverage of the Pamunkey's pursuit of federal recognition coverage was undertaken to discern the number of mainstream prints, online, and broadcast stories that were published, or aired, as well as the use of stereotypical phrases in that coverage, in the available databases through February 2018. It was expected most of mainstream stories would be framed as "casino" stories and not "tribal sovereignty" stories. It was also expected congressional hearing testimony would follow a similar pattern of the news media and focus on casinos and not tribal sovereignty.

A LexisNexis search for "news" related to the federal recognition of the Pamunkey Indian Tribe generated 244 print and online articles between 1987 and February 2018. The Tribe received recognition on July 15, 2015. This amounts to fewer than eight articles per year over thirty-one years. These 244 articles also represent the universe of articles published about the Tribe between 1985 and February 28, 2018, on any subject. Almost 40 percent (90) referenced gaming, and surprisingly, more stories (114) included sovereignty (46.7 percent). Only 10 stories included both.

The only broadcast story to air about the Pamunkey's federal recognition was on NPR's *All Things Considered* on July 2, 2015, right after the acknowledgment announcement.[9] In the entire indexed time, this was only one of two stories about the Pamunkey Tribe. The other aired on 6 KITV Honolulu, HI May 2, 2016. The story does not refer to the Pamunkey's new sovereign status, but it does report that "MGM Resorts opposed recognition because the company is building a new casino in Maryland across the Potomac River from Virginia and fears the Pamunkey might build their own gambling facility." None of the stereotypical words or phrases appeared during the indexed time. Between July 22, 1994 and July 2, 2015, there were nine congressional hearings about the Pamunkey Tribe. Two of those stories referenced gaming operations, and four included references to the tribe's status as a sovereign nation.

The Pamunkey's journey to federal recognition was long and arduous, and the news coverage surrounding the journey waxed and waned over time. To make sense of what the stories looked like during these cycles of recognition over the years, the articles were categorized by significant periods relating to the acknowledgement process. It begins with those articles that appeared prior to the Pamunkey Tribe seeking recognition through its official application (FAP); then when the first congressional bill for recognition was put forward, then when the bill moved to the Senate, then a period when the bill was stagnant and a new Congress was introduced, and finally the period immediately after it received recognition. There is an interspersing therefore, of the Tribe seeking recognition through the FAP and through the legislative process. This provides a broader understanding of how the agenda-setting function of the media was working throughout the recognition process.

Pre-Recognition to Recognition Sought Articles

The first and only article published that included the terms Pamunkey and federal recognition, or federal acknowledgment, prior to the Tribe seeking recognition was a 1987 profile about the Pamunkey chief, Tecumseh Deerfoot Cook.[10] The first story about the Pamunkey's pursuit of federal recognition was in 1994 in the Richmond Times-Dispatch.[11] Once the news of its pursuit of federal recognition gained traction in 1999, the number of stories increased, and nineteen stories were published through June 2000.

First Bill Introduced

In July 2000 Rep. James Moran (D-VA) introduced the first bill to the 106th Congress to federally recognize the Pamunkey Tribe. The story of the Pamunkey's decision to pursue federal recognition began to receive national coverage in September 2000 when Frank R. Wolf, of McLean VA, then a leading congressional opponent of the gambling industry, proposed a moratorium on the expansion of gaming. Wolf urged Virginians in a Washington Post editorial that federal recognition could exempt Tribes from state laws against casino gambling saying that "crime, bankruptcy, family breakup and death" are "compounded by the political corruption that gambling brings to local, state and federal government."[12] In the subsequent years, the bill stalled. Then, in March 2005, the Virginia Tribes began leveraging the upcoming 400-year anniversary of the founding of Jamestown. They threatened to boycott the celebration if they didn't receive recognition from the 109th Congress. The Tribes decided to use the event as a way to highlight their lack of acknowledgment by adopting the slogan, "First to Welcome, Last to be Recognized." During this five-year period, 63 articles were published.

Bill Moves to Senate

In May 2007, the House in the 110th U.S. Congress finally moved to recognize only six Tribes before moving the bill to the senate. The Pamunkey and Mattaponi were not included in that bill because both had reservations. The two Tribes refused to give up their gaming rights as the other Tribes were willing to do. During this two-year period, 33 articles were published.

Recognition on Hold to Recognition Received

In the seven years spanning June 2007 to July 2014, only 39 stories were published. In late 2014, when two factions rose up against the Pamunkey's pursuit of recognition, the stories started appearing again.

In November 2014, the Congressional Black Caucus called on the Obama Administration to block the Pamunkey's recognition because of the tribe's long history of banning interracial marriages. The law stated: "No member of the Pamunkey Indian Tribe shall intermarry with [any] nation except White or Indian under penalty of forfeiting their rights in Town." Pamunkey Chief Kevin Brown said that the law had been repealed in 2012 and had never been enforced—and, in fact, was part of the white supremacist practices of Walter Plecker's Racial Integrity Act that had prompted the original law. In order to adhere to the Act, the tribal members who intermarried could risk their children not being considered Pamunkey.

In March 2015, MGM Resorts International submitted a thirty-nine-page opposition to the recognition process as it was building the $925 million National Harbor Casino Resort along the Potomac River in Maryland, about 120 miles north of the Pamunkey Reservation.

Awaiting BIA Decision

During the six months that the Tribes awaited the BIA's decision (January 1, 2015–July 1, 2015), 17 articles were published.

Recognition Announced Articles

The BIA announced on July 2, 2015 that the Pamunkey Tribe's decades-long quest for recognition had been approved, making the Tribe the first in Virginia to receive the designation. Over the next ten days, 19 stories were published.

Post Recognition Articles

Between August 2, 2015 and January 1, 2016, 15 more stories were published. On the last day of a ninety-day window to appeal the BIA's decision to solidify the Pamunkey federal recognition, Stand Up for California (a one-person nonprofit organization run by Cheryl Schmit) filed a request for reconsideration to the Interior Board of Indian Appeals. That appeal failed and the Pamunkey Tribe's recognition stood.

Post Jordan Act Recognition Articles

Between February 1, 2016 and January 28, 2018, 38 more articles about the Pamunkey's recognition were published in the context of the coming recognition of the six Tribes seeking acknowledgment under the Jordan Act. The majority contain the gaming frame (73.7 percent) and about a quarter contained the sovereignty frame (26.3 percent).

Casinos, Gaming, and Sovereignty

Of the 244 stories about the Pamunkey and federal recognition, 90 (36.8 percent) included gaming references and more, 114 (46.7 percent), included sovereignty terms. Only 10 stories used both.[13] The majority of the stories (25.8

percent) were published in the five-year period after a bill was introduced in Congress that would have granted federal recognition. These articles also included the highest percent of references to gaming (85.7 percent) except during a six-month period in which the BIA was making its decision (88.2 percent). Of the 38 articles published after the federal recognition decision, 26 (65 percent) either were about, or included references to the six other Virginia Tribes seeking federal recognition through the legislative route. The Tribes had agreed to waive their right to operate gaming facilities in exchange for acknowledgment.

Between June 1, 2007 and December 31, 2014, the Pamunkey Tribe's pursuit of federal recognition was on hold. Only about 15 percent of the stories during this time focused on gaming and more focused on sovereignty, but only at the rate of other time periods (about 25 percent). In late 2014, the Congressional Black Caucus opposed the recognition because of the tribe's aforementioned ban on interracial marriage and six of the thirty-nine stories focused on that dissension. For three years prior, the Pamunkeys were not on the news agenda at all. Between February 20, 2011 and April 4, 2014, no stories were published. Only five were published in 2010 (and all in October) after the Tribe announced it was seeking recognition through the FAP. Therefore, no clear pattern emerges as to why gaming wasn't as prevalent a topic, except in the case of the opposition by the Black Caucus.

Between July 3, 2015 and January 30, 2018, mainstream print news published 39 articles that included references to the Pamunkey acknowledgment decision. During this time, the Pamunkey Tribe was recognized on July 2, 2015; the Thomasina E. Jordan Act was reintroduced two years later on March 21, 2017 by Senators Warner and Kaine to coincide with 400th anniversary of the burial of Pocahontas. The bill passed ten months later on January 30th. Only 38 percent of the 39 stories published contained the gaming frame, although fewer (25.6 percent) used the sovereignty frame. Given that the Tribes had agreed to forego gaming, the percent of stories that used gaming frames was still high, but it is possible that since federal recognition is so tied to gaming operations if it seems a Tribe will not be acknowledged, or acknowledgment is imminent, the connection fractures and reporters utilize other story frames. A deeper read into each story reveals a history frame. In 36 of the 39 stories, the reporting points to the importance of the six Tribes to the history of Virginia, particularly their role in ensuring the survival of the first permanent settlement in America. Headlines such as "An Identity Denied,"[14] "How a Long Dead White Supremacist Still Threatens the Future of Virginia's Indian Tribe,"[15] "400 Years Is Long Enough," and "Overdue Recognition: Six American Indian Tribes in Virginia Deserve to Be Acknowledged by the US"[16] introduce stories that place the Tribes in historical perspective to the United States and acknowledge the wrongs done to them for four centuries. The revival of the Pocahontas story could account for the use of the history frame during this time. But it is more likely that given the six Tribes were no longer an economic threat, that journalists chose to focus on the stories they should also have reported when gaming might have been a topic.

NEWS COVERAGE OF THE CHICKAHOMINY, THE EASTERN CHICKAHOMINY, THE UPPER MATTAPONI, THE RAPPAHANNOCK, THE MONACAN, AND THE NANSEMOND

The Thomasina E. Jordan Indian Tribes

The Thomasina E. Jordan Indian Tribes of Virginia Federal Recognition Act was signed by President Trump on January 29, 2018.[17] Ironically, Trump consistently denigrated Senator Elizabeth Warren by referring to her as "Pocahontas." The Tribes granted recognition by the Jordan Act were relatives of the Pamunkey Tribe, which Matoaka (Pocahontas), was a member. She was the daughter of Wahunsenacawh (Powhatan), the paramount chief of many of the tributary Tribes in the region. Thomasina E. Jordan, the former chairwoman of the Virginia Council of Indians and a member of the Mashpee Wampanoag Nation of Cape Cod, was an activist and advocate for Indigenous people. Although not a member of any of the Tribes seeking federal recognition, she was often the voice for them. She taught the Virginia Tribes how to maneuver in the political system, and was instrumental in legislation giving tribal members the ability to correct the racially inaccurate birth certificates processed by Walter Plecker.[18]

Originally, these six Tribes, along with the Mattaponi and Pamunkey, sought recognition as a group. However, since the Mattaponi and the Pamunkey Tribe had reservations and, therefore, a land resource they could potentially use for a gaming operation, they decided to pursue recognition through the FAP. The Mattaponi have yet to be recognized.

The timeline used to analyze articles about the Tribes that received recognition via the Jordan Act is similar to that used to examine the Pamunkey. News stories were categorized by significant periods relating to the federal recognition process beginning with any articles which appeared prior to the Tribes seeking recognition through the tribe's official application—and, next, when the first congressional bill for recognition was put forward and that bill moving to the Senate; then, the period when the Pamunkey Tribe was recognized; then, the introduction of the Jordan Act; then, the recognition period; and finally after the Tribes received recognition. As with the Pamunkey, the Tribes' different avenues of their search for acknowledgment are intermixed in the analysis.

A search for individual tribe's names and federal recognition resulted in 424 articles published between August 1987 and February 28, 2018. Of those, 368 were from newspapers, 52 from wire feeds and four blog posts (all from *The Washington Post*-online). None of the stereotypical phrases or words were used in the stories. In all but two time periods, gaming references accounted for more than half of the stories, ranging from 53 percent to 93 percent and in every time frame they were more prevalent than sovereignty references.

A LexisNexis search for all broadcast stories, news and other, which aired about using any of the six tribe's names and on any subject produced only 20 articles between September 2001 and January 11, 2018. None of the stories were broadcast news stories. A search for the Thomasina E. Jordan Indian Tribes of Virginia Federal Recognition Act produced no broadcast news results either.

Between September 29, 2015 and May 11, 2005, 17 congressional hearings occurred concerning the act. Eight of those stories referenced gaming operations and four included references to the tribes' status as sovereign Nations, and four had both.

Pre-Recognition to Recognition Sought Articles

Although some of Tribes began their pursuit of federal recognition in the 1970s, only three stories were indexed in the database until 1995. A Boston Globe article quoted a member of the Rappahannock Tribe attending a pow wow and also noted that one of the Wampanoag Tribes was seeking federal recognition.

Recognition Sought

In 1995 six of the Tribes (excluding the Pamunkey) expressed new interest in seeking federal recognition. Some applied for government funds, and some sent letters of intent to the BIA. However, after this, no more stories were published until four years later when the Virginia General Assembly passed a resolution for the recognition of the Tribes. Between June 1995 and June 2000, 36 stories were published.

First Bill Introduced

A bill to acknowledge the Tribes was introduced in July 2000 to the 106th Congress. In January 2001, the Mattaponi and the Pamunkey withdrew their bid for recognition. The bill sat in Senate and was never acted on. During this time period, 118 articles were published.

Bill Moves to Senate then Stalls

As the 400th anniversary of the founding if Jamestown approached, a new bill was sponsored in. Tribes had vowed to protest the 2007 celebration if they didn't receive recognition. In 2006, the Rappahannock requested a separate bill for their sole recognition in which it would forego any gaming rights. In April 2007, the other Tribes agreed to an amendment to the bill to forego their gaming rights as well. While the Tribes were in limbo between April 2005 and May 2007, 123 articles are published.

Thomasina E. Jordan Act Introduced

The Jordan Act was introduced by Rep. Jim Moran (D-VA) in July 2008. A year later, the house passed the bill. This was the 110th Congress. In 2014, it finally moved to a full Senate vote. This was the 114th Congress. The Tribes remained in limbo between June 2007 and March 2015 and 91 articles were published in the eight-year time span.

Pamunkey Tribe recognized through FAP

On July 2, 2015, the Pamunkey Tribe received federal recognition. Stories about the six other Tribes' pursuit of recognition were overshadowed by the news of the Pamunkey and four articles were published—all referencing the Pamunkey decision.

Six Tribes Recognized

Between the Pamunkey decision in July and the recognition through the Jordan Act on January 31, 2018, 39 stories were published. In September 2016, the House Natural Resources Committee voted to recognize the Virginia Tribes as part of a package of bills that, if successful, would have given Congress the ultimate authority to recognize Tribes. It died.

Senators Mark Warner (D-Va.) and Tim Kaine (D-Va.) reintroduced the Jordan Act to coincide with the 400th anniversary of Pocahontas' burial (March 21, 2017). Representative Rob Wittman (R-Va) introduced H.R. 984 on February 7, 2017. The bill passed the House by voice vote on May 17, 2017, and the Senate by unanimous consent on January 11, 2018, by the 115th Congress. Former president Trump signed the legislation into January

29, 2018. In the month that followed the recognition, 7 stories were published. Only one of those stories was not a recap of the passing of the act.

AGENDA SETTING AND THE VIRGINIA INDIANS

The agenda-setting role of news media focuses public attention on a news story. People prefer news that supports their beliefs and avoid news that does not.[19] Journalists are not immune to this as they report and write the news. So, although none of the Virginia Tribes originally intended to open gaming establishments, four decades of stories about the Pamunkey Tribe seeking federal recognition were framed as if it gets acknowledged, then it will open a casino. Perhaps that is why, in the end, the Pamunkey decided to pursue their own gaming operation.[20]

Although it was expected that congressional testimony would follow the pattern of the news media, it did not. This testimony was actually more likely to include references to sovereignty than to gaming operations. During congressional testimony, however, Tribes are allowed to speak for themselves. Thus, it is possible that tribal leaders were able to move conversations away from gaming and highlight their pursuit of the sovereign status that would afford them a one-to-one relationship with the government representatives that they were testifying to. Congressional leaders may have more knowledge about tribal relationships with the U.S. government, and so they could have been less likely to bring up gaming. This is an area that needs to be further examined.

Because Tribes continue to seek and receive federal recognition even in the face of negative mainstream news media coverage, it's difficult to tell how much influence the news media does actually have, if any, on the acknowledgment process. However, the results of the content analysis point to necessary training for journalists and editors to understand Indigenous people and issues such as federal recognition. It also highlights the importance of bias training for journalists and editors to face the hegemony underlying the reporting and editing process.

Some past training might have worked. Very few stories used stereotypical phrases and words, but an in-depth analysis of every story was not conducted. Even if newsrooms never really diversified, most journalists have received training in journalism school or elsewhere alerting them these terms are so overtly stereotypical that they do little to build or retain audiences.

The next step in examining news coverage is to investigate how Indigenous media can provide a route for journalists to take action to end centuries-long misrepresentation.

NOTES

1. The BIA has been accused of as being too bureaucratic and not always acting in the best interest of Tribes. For example, see Robertson, 2012 and Hunt, 2012.
2. Stannard, 1992.
3. Stannard, 1992.
4. Monocan Indian Nation, https://www.monacannation.com/our-history.html.
5. Rountree & Turner, 2002.
6. Wood, 1989.
7. Rountree & Turner, 2002.
8. Deal, 2014.
9. Naylor, 2015.
10. Green, 1987.
11. Latane, 1994.
12. Hsu, 2000.
13. In March 2018, the Pamunkey proposed a $700,000 gambling resort.
14. Heim, June 30, 2015.
15. Heim, July 2002.
16. Overdue Recognition, 2016, Sept 22.
17. H.R.984—115th Congress (2017–2018) Thomasina E. Jordan Indian Tribes of Virginia Federal Recognition Act of 2017.
18. Booker, 1999.
19. Iyengar & Hahn, 2009.
20. In January 2020, five years after the Pamunkey Indian Tribe received federal recognition, it signed a development agreement with the City of Norfolk, Virginia to build a $500M casino and hotel on 13.4 acres of city land. It has an expected opening date of 2023.

Chapter 9

Indigenous News Coverage of Federal Recognition

The media has, for its own purposes, created a false image of the Native American. Too many of us have patterned ourselves after that image. It is time now that we project our own image and stop being what we never really were.[1] —Gerald Wilkinson, National Indian Youth Council

The first Indigenous newspaper in the United States was printed on February 21, 1828, in New Echota, Cherokee Nation (in what is now Georgia) with Elias Boudinot as its editor. The bilingual English and Cherokee publication used the Cherokee syllabary created by Sequoyah.[2] Since then, Indigenous publications and broadcasts have told the stories of their communities to preserve history, celebrate community and have been used as an important source of information about sovereignty for Indigenous people.[3] *Let My People Know* in 2010 used a historical perspective to explore approaches early Indigenous journalists took to comprehend the cataclysmic changes taking place in their lives.[4] Centuries of negligence and stereotyping in media coverage of Indigenous people spurred Tribes to create their own news outlets.

Although the expansion of Indigenous journalism began in the 1970s,[5] it started thriving in the 1980s with the founding of the Native American Press Association in 1983 by a group of Indigenous journalists from around the country (now the Native American Journalists Association). NAJA's goal is to lift up Native voices in all platforms of media, and work with its colleagues across the media industry to ensure accurate and contextual reporting about Native people and communities.[6] The first Indigenous television network based in the United States launched in 2011, and by 2014 First Nations Experience was national.[7] Although there is only one weekly Native TV broadcast in the United States (*Indian Country Today*), more than 300 Indigenous digital and print publications and nearly 70 Indigenous radio programs broadcast daily from around the country.[8]

The combination of increased professionalism among Indigenous journalists, the economic growth in tribal communities, and a heightened sense of tribal sovereignty fueled by the income from tribal casinos[9] helped encourage this growth. Indigenous news sources play a vital role in informing their audiences about issues that affect their sovereignty[10] and their pursuit of federal recognition to gain sovereignty.

Ethnic News Watch indexes almost 500 ethnic and minority media organizations. The database was used to gather a sample of Indigenous news coverage of the federal recognition of Tribes. Ethnic News Watch defines Indigenous media as, "those media or forms of media where expression is created, owned, controlled, and managed by Indigenous Peoples to produce and exchange culturally appropriate information in the languages that they speak and understand."[11]

The database contains full texts of newspapers and magazines of ethnic and minority media outlets from 1959 to present that give researchers access to crucial perspectives often left out of the mainstream. The initial search only included the terms "federal recognition" or "federal acknowledgment" because the search was limited to U.S. Indigenous news sources and American Indian or Native American would be implied, or the specific name of a Tribe would have been used. There were 27 possible newspapers (see Appendix C for a list of Indigenous news sources)[12] and magazines and 23 of them had articles found in the search. The same period of all-indexed stories to February 18, 2018, was used as it was in the previous searches. 1,170 news articles were included in the analysis with the first appearing August 31, 1975. The majority (96.5 percent) of the stories were published in newspapers (1,130) and 40 in News from Native California, which was a magazine published out of Berkeley, CA.

It is important to list the news sources and their publication history, when it could be located, to understand how diverse and widespread Indigenous news sources are. These media outlets as well as the areas they serve, and their publishing history (when available),[13] and the number of articles that appeared in that source are listed below.

Indian Country Today, 599 articles
> A nonprofit news organization that covers tribes and Native people throughout the Americas through both digital and public broadcast platforms.[14]

Native American Times (magazine), 93 articles
   Launched in 1994 as the *Oklahoma Indian Times* and published bi-weekly, the Cherokee-serving publication was distributed throughout Oklahoma until 2014, when it went digital only.
Ojibwe News/Native American Press, 73 articles
   The *Ojibwe News* was founded in 1988 in 1991 merged with Native American Press and served the Ojibway Tribe of Minnesota.
Seminole Tribune, 61 articles
   The official newspaper of the Seminole Tribe of Florida, published monthly with a circulation of 4,000. It was first published as the Seminole News in 1956.
News from Indian Country, 55 articles
   A newspaper located on the Lac Courte Oreilles Ojibwe Reservation in Northern Wisconsin from 1986 until 2020.
The Circle: News from an American Indian Perspective, 42 articles
   A monthly publication out of Minneapolis, Minnesota since 1980.
News from Native California, 40 articles
   A quarterly magazine published since 1987.
Pequot Times, 38 articles
   A publication of the Mashantucket Pequot Nation of Connecticut since 1992.
Char-Koosta News, 39 articles
   The official news publication of the Flathead Indian Reservation, Salish and Kootenai Tribes, weekly since 1956.
Sho-Ban News, 27 articles
   Weekly newspaper of the Shoshone-Bannock Tribe located in Fort Hall, Idaho since 1970.
Cherokee Advocate, 15 articles
Cherokee Observer, 14 articles
   A newspaper published in Parkhill, Ok since 1933.
Cherokee Phoenix, 14 articles
   First printed in 1828 and continues to the present in both Cherokee and English.
Navajo Times, 6 articles
   Known during the early 1980s as Navajo Times Today, this newspaper was created by the Navajo Tribal Council in 1959 and in 1982 was the first daily newspaper owned and published by a Native American Indian Nation.
Wind River News, 6 articles
   A weekly publication covering news from the Eastern Shoshone and Northern Arapaho Tribe on the Wind River Indian Reservation in Wyoming since 1983.
Red Sticks Press, 5 articles
   A quarterly newspaper in St. Petersburg, Florida published beginning in 1994.

Au-Authm Action News, 3 articles
   A newspaper from the Salt River Pima-Maricopa Indian Community in Scottsdale, Arizona.
Oklahoma Indian Times, 3 articles
   A newspaper published in Afton, Oklahoma from 1995-2001.
The Native Nevadan, 3 articles
   The official newspaper of the Inter-Tribal Council of Nevada from 1965 to 1982.
Tundra Times, 3 articles
   The voice of Alaska Natives from 1962 to 1997.
Fort Apache Scout, 1 article
   The official newspaper of the White Mountain Apache Tribe of the Fort Apache Indian Reservation since 1962.
Ojibwe Akiing, 1 article
   A special section in *News from Indian Country* from Hayward Wisconsin published since 1996.
The Cherokee Voice, 1 article
   No publication information available.

Most of the federal recognition stories in these sources in late 1970s and early 1980s were published as news briefs without any reporting using sources. However, beginning with a story in *Indian Country Today* in November 1983, five years after the criteria were formally established, Indigenous news sources began more in-depth coverage of what federal recognition meant for Tribes. That story was about the Mashantucket Pequot Indian Tribe, and it quoted tribal chairman Richard Hayward, "Finally we have the opportunity to move ahead with our own plans to improve our day-to-day existence for our people."[15] The year before was the first mention of Indian gaming found in the search. The brief in *Sho-Ban News* was about the Shakopee Mdewakanton Sioux Tribe's (Minnesota) plans for high stakes bingo. A year later, the same newspaper published another brief about the Arizona House of Representatives passing a bill to regulate bingo on Indian reservations.

The Indigenous media search for stories that included references to Indian gaming found 536 articles, 519 in newspapers and 17 in magazines. The term sovereign or sovereignty appeared in 545 (47 percent) results (520 newspapers and 25 magazines) and within that search 300 (55 percent) articles also included gaming. Within the 654 articles that referenced gaming, 563 of them included one of the following terms, or a derivative of the term: culture, legal, history or economy. These terms imply sovereignty as Indigenous publications expect their audiences to understand the connection between gaming and sovereignty, and so do not always need to explicitly state it. A 2002 *Indian Country Today* article headlined "Let the Games Begin: Anti-Gamers

Rail Against Recognition; A Threat to Tribal Economics" encapsulates the importance of gaming to Tribes:

> While gaming is certainly not a panacea, it has become the most successful means of economic self-determination throughout Indian country. If Connecticut's anti-casino crowd is genuinely concerned about the welfare of the state's tribes, perhaps they might suggest some viable economic alternatives to casinos that will allow tribes to house, educate, employ and provide medical care for their members.[16]

Another good example of the difference in the context of articles that Indigenous media publish about federal recognition versus those published by the mainstream media was "Tribes find opposition to gambling the latest barrier to federal recognition,"[17] a headline from *News from Indian Country* in 2016. The story reports on the nuances of federal recognition from the tribal perspective and includes the legal, historical, cultural, and economic complications of the process.

A 2017 story from the *Seminole Tribune* provided the type of context that mainstream stories often lack. The excerpt is long, but it illustrates the importance of including history in stories about federal recognition.

> In 1817, U.S. General Edmund Gaines attacked the Mikasuki settlement at Fowltown and effectively declared war on the Seminóles. The resultant reign of destruction in north Florida, carried out by men commanded by Andrew Jackson was short-lived but brought with it unimaginable loss. Countless Seminóles lost their homes, their families, and their lives in this brutal raid. For those who endured, it was another push in the direction ever southward toward the sanctuary of the swamps where a core group would survive against impossible odds. Sixty years ago, in 1957, after years of struggling and facing the termination of U.S. government services, descendants of the survivors of Jackson's raid were federally recognized.[18]

A final example from the *Char-Koosta News* also illustrates the importance of history, as well as telling the story of the difficulty a Tribe has in proving it is actually a Tribe.

These requirements were difficult to meet for the Little Shell Tribe of Chippewa Indians of Montana. First, the Tribe is composed of people of mixed Indigenous and European descent. In Canada, such people are constitutionally recognized as Métis, but the United States offers no comparable legal status. Second, hundreds of Little Shell people were forcibly evicted from Montana under the Cree Deportation Act of 1896. This law, which followed a disputed treaty in 1863 and a fraudulent agreement in 1892, scattered the Little Shell across the West and into Alberta, Canada, producing unavoidable gaps in their ability to provide the documentation required in the federal recognition criteria. Finally, the only people interested in verifying their complicated history were the Little Shell themselves, leaving the Tribe with few options for third-party advocates.[19]

INDIGENOUS NEWS COVERAGE OF THE SIX VIRGINIA TRIBES

Ethnic News Watch indexed 41 newspaper articles that contained any of the names of the six Tribes (the Chickahominy, the Eastern Chickahominy, the Rappahannock, the Monacan, the Nansemond and, the Upper Mattaponi). The majority were published in *Indian Country Today 33* (08.4 percent). The *Native American Times*, *Seminole Tribune*, and *Wind River News* each published two stories. The *Navajo Times* and *The Circle* each published one article. *Indian Country Today* referenced gaming just over half (21) of the 41 articles (51.2 percent) and the terms sovereign or sovereignty appeared in eight of those articles.

The first story that included the word gaming in the search wasn't published until 2005 in a *Wind River News* story about the upcoming 400th celebration of the founding of Jamestown mentioned earlier in this book, and the story made the Tribes' stance on gaming clear from the beginning of the story:

> Tribal leaders are threatening to turn their participation in the upcoming Jamestown anniversary events into a protest if they don't get federal recognition by 2007. But the main sticking point to that recognition is casino gambling—something those Tribes insist they don't even want.[20]

The final story published within the time frame occurred in 2007 in *The Circle*. The last sentence of the story reads: "Bill language adopted at the committee level would bar the tribes from launching gaming operations. The provision was key to the measure's passage, lawmakers said."[21]

NOTES

1. Extracted from Wilkinson, 1974. With permission of the American Indian Digital History Project, https://www.aidhp.com/

2. It took Sequoyah twelve years to develop the syllabary, which was adopted by the Cherokee Nation in 1821 (Cushman, 2011). (For more info, see CherokeePhoenix.org (2015). History of the *Cherokee Phoenix*. [Accessed March 5, 2021, by this

author at http://www.cherokeephoenix.org/archives/history-of-the-cherokee-phoenix/article_30c25bf9-bc26-5628-9687-75e1be8581ba.html]).
3. Loew & Mella, 2005.
4. Murphy, 2010.
5. See Littlefield & Parins, 1984.
6. See najanewsroom.com.
7. Pollard, 2020.
8. Pollard, 2020.
9. Loew & Mella, 2005.
10. Loew & Mella, 2005.
11. Sunuwar, 2019, para. 1.
12. The list includes thirty-two publications, but five of them are indexed twice depending on date range.
13. The dates were referenced from the Library of Congress if they were not available through tribal sources. Additionally, not all publication information was able to be verified.
14. Today, ICT is a nonprofit and multiplatform news organization. It has also been both private and for-profit and tribally owned and for-profit.
15. *Indian Country Today*, 1983.
16. Wanamaker, 2002.
17. Wiltz, 2016.
18. Backhouse, 2017.
19. Furshong, 2016.
20. *Wind River News*, 2005.
21. *The Circle*, 2007.

Chapter 10

Perspectives from Native Journalists and Legal Experts on Covering Federal Recognition

Indigenous Standpoint Theory in Action

> In daily deadline journalism, you ask somebody what federal acknowledgement of a Tribe is going to mean. Probably the simplest and most obvious answer is gaming. —Dan Lewerenz, NARF staff attorney and former NAJA president.[1]

Mainstream media should follow the lead of Indigenous journalism outlets when they cover Tribes seeking federal recognition, as well as when they cover any issues about Indian Country or Indigenous people. And mainstream media should actively hire Indigenous journalists to truly fulfill their obligations to fairly and accurately cover all of their communities, or as Tristan Ahtone (Kiowa) editor-at-large at Grist put it, "You're not serving your audience if you don't have somebody who covers Indigenous communities. If your newsroom is ignoring Indigenous voices or expertise in covering Indigenous communities, it's hard to hide the sort of colonial nature of your news outlet."[2]

This chapter uses interviews with Indigenous journalists to provide a roadmap for non-Indigenous journalists to increase media literacy about news coverage of Indian Country and Indigenous people. The Indigenous journalists were asked questions pertaining to four areas of coverage: frames and perspective, sourcing, structure, and advice to non-Indigenous journalists. The journalists were: Bryan Pollard, Citizen of Cherokee Nation, project manager for news partnerships at the *Associated Press*, former associate director of the Native American Journalists Association (NAJA), past president of the Native American NAJA, and former editor of the *Cherokee Phoenix*; Deb Krol, Xolon Salinan, currently one of two Indigenous affairs reporters at the Arizona Republic; Patty Talahongva, Hopi, past president of NAJA and Executive Producer of *Indian Country Today*; Paula Peters,

Wampanoag, public relations and new media pundit for SmokeSygnals; and Dan Lewerenz, Iowa Tribe of Kansas and Nebraska, now a NARF staff attorney, a former *Associated Press* reporter between 1997 and 2007, and a former president of NAJA. These Indigenous journalists and one former journalist, have decades of journalism experience among them.

FRAMING

When reporters look at federal recognition there's very little coverage because no one understands that story, Patty Talahongva said.[3] The local media might be covering it because it is impacting their community. The big draw for the story will be casinos if a Tribe has a casino planned because that seems to be one industry that everyone thinks is going to make money. They don't understand how expensive it is to go into casino gaming, Talahongva said, adding many of the casino operators and management are not Native and although there is a Native hiring preference, those jobs tend to be the low-paying ones. "There's so many contradictions when it comes to Indian gaming. Who really is benefiting? I can't think of a single national story, broadcast story about the Lumbee's federal recognition and why the Eastern Band (of Cherokee Indians) is so opposed to them." She believes that the reason the Mashapee Wampanoag got federal recognition coverage is because the Tribe is associated with greeting the pilgrims and so people can understand that connection. "The nuances are definitely not covered because there are so many layers. I think that Americans at large still think of us as one group of people. They don't get the fact that we have our own languages, our own cultures, our own religions. We are not just 'Indians.'"

Talahongva added that traditional Native governments are also cause for much of the ignorance surrounding recognition. Traditional matrilineal governments are at odds with the patriarchal American government, but many tribal governments were set up by the American government in ways that conflicted with original cultures. "So, it's really hard to understand the layers. At Hopi we are very layered. Every village has a whole 'spreadsheet' of leadership. And each village is autonomous. Even though we are all Hopi, we have three dialects, and some villages might not have the traditional forms of government that my village at First Mesa does, or the villages at Second Mesa."

Lewerenz[4] expanded on this adding that federal acknowledgment does not lend itself to daily journalism, and that news audiences have very little understanding of Native issues. "Journalism requires a lot of process and needs to begin as an exercise in explanatory journalism. It's particularly problematic when a reporter is assigned to a story on a tight deadline and attempts to simplify a story with which they are not familiar. That's when things go wrong," he said, because "coverage of federal acknowledgement is often a conflict between the seeming need to cover what looks like news, and the lack of knowledge" about the process.

Bryan Pollard[5] sees the stark difference between how Indigenous media cover federal recognition versus how mainstream media covers it as one of different paradigms. "Tribal media is going to approach federal recognition from a political perspective. They understand that they have political identity, and that identity is the underpinning of their sovereignty and their ability to be a self-determining Indigenous people." The paradigm of the mainstream media is that Native people have a racialized status. It's a status that has to do with the power relationship between Tribes and state governments and the federal government. "Stories are not covered in the same way that other countries are covered, which would be a recognition of sovereignty," Pollard said.

This type of coverage seeks to educate the audience on how federal recognition will be part of the political identity of a Tribe that will enable them to develop their economic and cultural impact. But, because the mainstream media only understands Indigenous identity as a racialized one, it doesn't cover the political aspect of federal recognition. "Coverage by mainstream media reinforces stereotypes and tropes and can't escape the racialized paradigm of federal recognition" Pollard said. Until it does, it won't be able to view Indigenous people through their inherent sovereign political identity. Nor do reporters understand tribal government. Talahongva said that this is because "America's children are still not taught any decent amount of American Indian government." And even if they are taught, it's only Tribes in their states. To complicate it further, some states may only have two Tribes, but other states have many. And some states may have had Tribes, but they were removed. If the Tribes were removed, there may not be a mandate for public education on the Tribes. So, the local government structure cannot be applied nationwide. "It doesn't fit" she said. "We have this big gap in education and understanding. Whether it's teaching about Indians in the past, or teaching about Indians currently no one is taught federal Indian law." What's concerning is that it's not just journalists who don't understand tribal governments; local, state, and national legislatures don't either. "It goes all the way to the Supreme Court."

According to Deb Krol,[6] it's difficult to get reporters to divorce casinos from recognition. And it's also difficult to navigate both the bureaucracy and arcane rules of federal recognition. For example, Krol said, "Unless you were on the BIA list before 1934, or you have some other way of obtaining trust land in order to have a casino you have to have a reservation." So, Tribes that go through the process using an act of Congress are less likely to have the ability to open a casino. Recognition is also very difficult unless Tribes have money and lobbyists working for them in Washington, she said. In 2015, when the BIA changed the criteria for recognition, it acknowledged that "if they were to put all the [non-recognized] Tribes through this process, only 25% would make it."

Krol notes that only one California Tribe has successfully gone through the process, and that the differences in these processes are confusing for any journalist. The Timbisha Shoshone Tribe of Death Valley, CA, for example, was officially recognized in 1983, but did not receive a land base until November 1, 2000,[7] when the Timbisha Homeland Act was signed into law by President William J. Clinton[8] sanctioning the transfer of more than 7,700 acres of land in California and Nevada to the Tribe.[9] She said the tribe's application was only sixty pages.

Talahongva sees the news as only being interested in feathers and casinos and not interested in the layers of history that come with federal recognition. But casinos shouldn't be an issue even if a Tribe does want one because America is based on a free-enterprise system. The difference is that by law, the majority of Tribes have to share their casino revenue. "Tribes are the only businesses and governments that are required to share their revenue. Non-Indian casinos do not have to share their revenue. Tribal gaming operations do not get tax breaks under the guise of creating jobs. There are no stories about this."

SOURCING

It is highly probable that mainstream reporters do not understand the inner workings of tribal government. Therefore, they may not go beyond sourcing the obvious elected officials who represent the legislative part of tribal government and who can provide a political perspective of federal recognition, such as tribal chairpersons and tribal council members. The staff who make the Tribes operate do so even as political leaders change; they are more likely to understand the logistics of what has happened, and what will happen in the federal recognition process from a practical perspective. Krol said they would make good sources.

Krol added Tribes that have gone through the process are also good sources of information for stories, and particularly Tribes that have tried and failed, but also Tribes that have been successful. It is important to understand how much money they have spent and how long it has taken them in the process. Talahongva added to this saying that reporters should talk to Tribes that have not had to go through the process. In addition to talking to tribal council members and lawyers, reporters should embed themselves and talk to community members. "A lot of times elders get left out because reporters don't understand how real tribal leadership works, that a lot of times it is the elders who are running things by giving council and advice," Krol said. She added that reporters leave out women, and reporters need to cultivate women and elders and not expect to be able to drop in and have them want to talk. Talahongva's perspective on why women are left out is because from the beginning of the formation of the United States, the founders couldn't grasp the concept that women held leadership roles because many tribal governments are matrilineal, and the American government is a patriarchal government.

Other avenues of sourcing are available that journalists often fail to utilize. Talahongva recommends that the Native American Rights Fund (NARF) be utilized as a source.[10] NARF is the oldest, largest nonprofit legal organization defending the rights of Native American Tribes, organizations, and people. Krol recommended "people who have no stake in the game." By this, she means lawyers who aren't representing the Tribes, or any opposition, ethnographers who may provide context about roadblocks to proving tribal lineage and former Bureau of Indian Affairs employees who can offer insight into the bureaucracy. To get away from the controversy, and in addition to including elders and women as sources, Krol recommended non-Indigenous reporters create source lists that include lawyers and lobbyists.

But reporters should also be paying attention to the social media Tribes have embraced to put their messages out. Talahongva says, Tribes can now shape their narrative about who they are and this can help reporters understand tribes' perspectives.

STRUCTURE

"They are all trying to do something better for their people and for their future generations," Talahongva said about her approach to covering federal recognition. Acknowledgment reaffirms sovereignty that enables Tribes to reinforce economic structures. If Tribes do have, or want casinos, Indigenous media cover the Tribes from the perspective of job creation and economic stability for its citizens. Economic stability bolsters the coffers that can provide better healthcare and better education and the funds available to reaffirm culture through programs such as language and elder programs. "The *Cherokee Phoenix* focuses on the upside rather than the downside of casinos," Pollard said, because of the money casinos give the government for its citizens. But Pollard said that mainstream media covers "the three Cs: casinos, corruption and controversy." He said that the casino coverage he does see is about how they are going to attract crime, which he says also is often the view of tribal citizens. But the citizens of the Cherokee Nation understand the world-class health care available to them wouldn't be available without the casinos. So Indigenous media include this perspective.

Talahongva approaches stories for *Indian Country Today* with the perspective that the audience already gets it. "And if you don't understand it, that's on you to look it up." But the mainstream media never move beyond the potential criminal or controversial aspect of casinos, Pollard said. Krol adds that mainstream media concentrates on the money aspect and not the fact the federal recognition will allow Tribes to "bring their burial objects home, bring their funerary and cultural objects home, allow them to access ICWA [Indian Child Welfare Act] regulations and to protect elders, and educate their kids how [Tribes] see fit." It doesn't focus on the diversification that federal recognition, with or without casinos, can bring.

Krol said the same tropes that non-Indigenous reporters apply to general reporting on Indian Country "apply doubly to federal recognition. They always want to have a picture of a Native person doing a ceremony, singing, drumming, dancing, because singing around the campfire is what being an Indian is all about." Conversely, Indigenous media are more likely to focus on the issues more pertinent to the Tribes, issues like housing, as Krol relates in a story about the Federated Indians of Graton Rancheria, a federation of Coast Miwok and Southern Pomo groups in rural Northern California,[11] who wanted townhouses. The surrounding community accused the tribes of "going to trash cars and trash houses" and violating the rural landscape. The mainstream media should have taken the time to ask the Tribes why they decided on the type of housing they did in a notoriously expensive area of Santa Rosa, California, instead of reporting only on the outcry from the surrounding community. "The Tribes only had 10 acres to build on, and townhouses fit the budget to make sure it served the Tribes' needs." The context of the mainstream media is what the Tribes are going to do to the non-Indigenous community residing near the Tribes, versus the Indigenous perspective of this is what Tribes can do given the circumstances that they have been dealt. The focus of the mainstream is the destruction of the white community when the Indians are allowed to come into their space.

ADVICE TO NON-INDIGENOUS JOURNALISTS AND MEDIA

Each of the Indigenous journalists interviewed stressed the importance of reporters needing to do homework prior to jumping on a story about federal recognition. Talahongva says the first place they should look is the Constitution, because "Indians are the only race that's mentioned in it." Those who do stories on federal recognition should know that Article I,

Section 8 of the Constitution identifies Tribes as sovereign political entities. It reads: "The Congress shall have Power To regulate Commerce with foreign Nations, and among the several States, and with the Indian Tribes."

But knowing this doesn't just mean learning what sovereignty is and why Tribes have it. "Homework means context and the understanding that this isn't an event that just popped up," Pollard said. The federal recognition process has a context of "hundreds of years" behind what is happening with the current story. Krol agreed that reporters who are covering federal recognition need to take the time and read the history and the criteria. They should also revisit Tribes that have received federal recognition and ask how they have benefited. From Krol's perspective, areas that have had a Tribe become federally recognized realize that their fears never came to fruition. Reporters should go back and ask those interviewed in the stories leading up to federal recognition their current perspective. In most cases, she said, "the hue and cry will have died down because the Tribe has ended up being a really good neighbor." She notes that Tribes are able to bring in services like firefighters that serve the entire community, not just the Tribe. Reporters only go back to a federal recognition story if there is a controversy associated with it.

Without the context of the history of a tribal group's reason for seeking federal recognition, "it can't be taken lightly if you want to cover the story seriously," Pollard said, "and specifically you need to look at treaties." Treaties are important legal documents that are already in place. Pollard said even though the federal government and the media have ignored them for years, and that they are old, they are key to many stories. Those working in Indigenous media don't often mention treaties,[12] but the knowledge is also implied.

Pollard says a good example of this is the No DAPL protests. "There was no coverage of the treaty rights that the protesters were there to uphold."[13] And, there was no coverage about the fact that much of the lands were disputed. "They were lands that were never ceded by the Tribe," but that the federal government just took as belonging to it, Pollard said. However, just relying on treaties only works for Tribes that have them. "Only two-thirds of Tribes have treaties," Krol said. It's important for non-Indigenous journalists to also understand the history and origins of treaties, which is why a short explanation is offered here.

The first peace treaty in what was to become the United States was signed in October 1646 between the General Assembly of Virginia and Necotowance of the Pamunkey Tribe who was Paramount Chief of the Powhatan Confederacy. The treaty established a relationship between the coastal plains Algonquin and the English settlers of Virginia.[14] The remaining Tribes of the decimated Powhatan Confederacy and other coastal Tribes became tributaries to the King of England and were required to pay a yearly tribute to the Virginia governor, which they still do today. Thirty years later, the second Treaty of 1677 (the Treaty Between Virginia and The Indians, and also known as the Treaty of Middle Plantation)[15] expanded the tributary Tribes to include Siouan and Iroquoian speakers.[16] It wasn't until almost 200 years later when the first Tribes between the presently existing U.S. and Native Tribes would be signed. In September 1778, the United States established its first treaty with the Delaware Tribe. In the 1851 Treaty of Fort Laramie, the United States acknowledged the lands of the Cheyenne, Sioux, Arapaho, Crow, Assiniboine, Mandan, Hidatsa, and Arikara Nations constituted Indian territory and did not claim any part of it.[17] The United States recognized Tribes' existence as distinct, sovereign entities and established a model of the 371 ratified treaties to follow, until 1871.[18]

Focusing on the humanity of Indigenous communities as part of the federal recognition process and those who stand to suffer or benefit, instead of the perceived controversy, is going to mean stories that are more fair and more accurate. Talahongva reminds journalists that every story is about somebody. "When you come across a Native person who is drunk on the street, what do you see? Do you see the hundreds of years of oppression in that person? Do you see the missed opportunities because he wasn't given opportunities? What do you see? Who is that person and what do they represent? Because for us, our tragedy is layered. And it's like a family heirloom that's passed down. Where's the American dream for them?"

"Mainstream media don't seem to have much of an issue with that when they are covering white people," Pollard said. By focusing on the humanity, media can create connections between people who are from different backgrounds so that they can empathize. Talahongva considers federal recognition as validation, and people have the need to be validated.

What's the number one reason they are seeking federal recognition? What are the perspectives of the different tribal members? These are critical questions to ask when reporting a story. For instance, for a generational perspective, Talahongva recommends acquiring the "youth voice" because they are the ones who are going to inherit the legacy of recognition. Once a Tribe gets federal recognition someone is going to have to step up and serve in those leadership roles. It's important to learn the questions to ask and having Indigenous journalists on mainstream news staffs can ensure fair and accurate reporting.

Krol is one of an affinity group of Indigenous affairs reporters in a Gannett newsroom around the country. Greg Burton,[19] executive editor of the Arizona Republic, said Gannett is dedicated to reporting on underserved communities and that this is part of the effort, and the industry realizes it doesn't look like the communities that they serve, and so they don't cover those communities. "If I'm in Arizona and I'm not writing for the Indigenous communities, I'm failing," he said. The infrastructure of the Indigenous desk enables the reporters to talk to each other about potential stories, share ideas, support each other with sources, and then potentially coordinate project coverage that could have a large impact. "But it's not a monolithic approach. What's going to work in one community isn't necessarily an issue in another community," Burton said. Burton has utilized grants available through Report for America[20] to help fund these critical staff positions.

One of Burton's first bosses was Mark Trahant (Shoshone-Bannock), an award-winning journalist who is now the editor of Indian Country Today and was a former president of the NAJA. Trahant has worked as an editor at both Indigenous and mainstream news outlets. He mentored Burton, and so, was instrumental in his understanding about covering Indigenous communities as a young journalist.

Burton's story is important because without that early mentorship, he may not have gone on to lead efforts to diversify the newsrooms that he worked in by adding Indigenous voices. This is also true of James Kinsella,[21] the business editor from 1983 to 2002 at the *Cape Cod Times* (a weekly publication with a subscription base of between 40,000 and 50,000 according to Kinsella) who covered the federal recognition of the Mashpee Wampanoag Tribe from 2000 to 2002. He said he learned a lot from Paula Peters about the Wampanoag, "she was my window into their world" that gave him perspective. "I wasn't aware of a lot of stuff until I began talking with Paula," he said.

Paula Peters is a modern traditional citizen of the Mashpee Wampanoag Tribe, and owner of SmokeSygnals, a creative consulting company, along with a Native American gift shop called the Wampanoag Trading Post and Gallery.[22] Peters was the first Native American staff writer at the *Cape Cod Times* where she worked between 1992 and 2002; she was the only Indigenous reporter in New England involved in NAJA at that time. Her father was the chairman of the Mashpee Tribe—who call themselves the People of the First Light[23]—when it filed a lawsuit to recover trust land; that conflict of interest kept her from covering her tribe's pursuit of federal recognition. However, she provided the newspaper staff with sources and context about the federal recognition process. "The newspaper was a better reflection of the overall community and inclusive of the Wampanoag because I was there," Peters said. She also said that the reporters actively came to her to get her perspective because they had the desire to know what was happening in their community.

The Mashpee Wampanoag Tribe was acknowledged in 2007 after a thirty-year process. Like some Tribes of the Powhatan Confederacy, Indian legends were built on stories of the Tribes of the Wampanoag because of their association with the Pilgrims, the first Thanksgiving, and the Plymouth Colony, an English Colony in what is now Cape Cod (Southeastern Massachusetts) from 1620 to 1691. "The federal acknowledgement process is the most cumbersome, bureaucratic legal litmus process known to man, and no other group of people is held to that standard," Peters said. Additionally, she said, without federal acknowledgment, it would have been difficult to have those lands returned to the Tribe.

Ironically, due to its pursuit of federal recognition to recover ancestral lands, corporate gaming developers courted the Mashpee tribal government in an attempt to gain access to gaming development on Cape Cod, but then the Tribe had to relinquish its right to sue for the return of its ancestral homelands. And fifteen years later, no casino has been built and the Tribe owes $440 million[24] to its investors.[25] Meanwhile, the Tribe also has an annual payment of $530,000 in lieu of taxes to the city of Taunton, where 151 acres are in trust for the Mashpee Tribe. This was supposed to be covered by gaming revenue.[26] "The process and the result of the process makes me feel like we are even more colonized," Peters said.

The Little Shell Tribe's process of federal recognition is another example of casino investors inserting themselves into the federal recognition process. By 2007, NARF had spent twenty-nine years and more than 3,400 attorney hours on the federal recognition of the Little Shell Tribe of Chippewa Indians of Montana. The cost at that time was already in excess of $1 million[27] including attorney time and the experts hired to do the technical work. It was finally recognized as part of the National Defense Authorization Act in 2020,[28] but only after twelve years of Montana Senator John Tester introducing the bill each year beginning in 2007.

The Mashpee Tribe did not have the financial resources to pursue federal recognition on its own and realized, after watching other Tribes that had petitioned after them be recognized, the path forward was aligning itself with a gaming backer to pay for all of the costs of the federal recognition process. The cost of gathering the documentary evidence is one of the main complaints about the federal recognition process.[29] And the cost inherently encourages outside backers.[30] It is not the "panacea of money raining from the sky," Peters said.

Representing a Tribe on acknowledgment is an incredibly labor-intensive task without a guarantee of compensation and so almost requires a nonprofit law firm because most unrecognized groups cannot pay for the necessary extensive legal services, Lewerenz said. For example, the Office of Federal Acknowledgment (OFA) suggested that in order to reverse its non-recognition determination that the Gay Head (Aquinnah) Wampanoag Tribe "produce the telephone bills of all their tribal members so they could document over time, the frequency and the scope to which they talk to each other," Arlinda Locklear,[31] an attorney for NARF who represented the Tribe at the time, said.

Lewerenz also noted that there was a great deal of leeway for the OFA to provide technical assistance under the old regulations. For instance, a group might provide its genealogical records and the reviewers might give them advice on what is missing and what it should look for. "But there was nothing that said here is what a completed petition looks like, or that it was complete," he said. So, there is no guide for other Tribes. As stated earlier in this book, the second step of the review process is that the OFA sends a letter assigning a petition number. But Tribes don't always follow up. Lewerenz said that this has resulted in the news media reporting the number of Tribes that have been waiting for decades without any action on their petition, when in fact, it is missing what happens in between.

"There are dozens of groups whose only communication with the Department of the Interior was to say that 'We want to be acknowledged,' and then there's a response from the Department of the Interior, and then there's no follow up." Under the old system, those were counted as open petitions. Under the new system, they are not. A number of reasons might stall or stop the process, including money, the burden of the task, or a recognition that the decision would most likely be negative. Under the old system, any of these reasons make it "look like the petition was opened 40 years ago," Lewerenz said. Under the new system, there are formalized steps until a petition is certified. "That's when it considers a group a new case and a new petitioner." These are seemingly small details that journalists should be aware of.

NOTES

1. Dan Lewerenz interview.
2. Yahr, 2021.
3. Patty Talahongva interview.
4. Dan Lewerenz interview.
5. Bryan Pollard interview.
6. Deb Krol interview. Krol is part of a new group of reporters at Gannet covering Tribes that share information for the network of news that goes across the country.
7. Catton, 2009.
8. Timbisha Shoshone Homeland Act into law. *Id*. at 88.
9. Timbisha Shoshone Tribe website.
10. According to the NARF website, in 1970 with funding from the Ford Foundation, California Indian Legal Services—one of the federally funded legal services programs serving California Indians—implemented a pilot project to provide legal services to Indians on a national level. That project became known as the Native American Rights Fund.
11. Federated Indians of Graton Rancheria website https://gratonrancheria.com/ Accessed February 2, 2021.

12. 315 of the articles in the Indigenous media search included the term treaty or treaties.

13. A search of stories in ProQuest U.S. Newsstream resulted in 629 articles that included "Dakota Access Pipeline and "treaty" or "treaties" between Nov. 2015 and March 2021. The same search in Ethnic News Watch found 45 results between August 2015 and January 2018.

14. Shefveland, 2016.

15. Preston, 2009.

16. Shefveland, 2016.

17. The 1868 Treaty of Fort Laramie was an agreement between Dakota, Lakota, and Nakota (Sioux Tribe) and the Arapaho that established the Great Sioux Reservation, a large expanse of lands west of the Missouri River. The treaty also designated the Black Hills as "unceded Indian Territory" for the exclusive use of the Tribe. However, when gold was discovered in the Black Hills, the United States broke the treaty and redrew the boundaries (Cutlip, 2018).

18. Kappler, 1904; Quinn, 1990.

19. Greg Burton interview.

20. Report for America's mission is "to strengthen our communities and our democracy through local journalism that is truthful, fearless, fair and smart." Report for America, https://www.reportforamerica.org/. It is an initiative of GroundTruth's where the mission is to restore journalism from the ground up by supporting the next generation of journalists through field reporting that serves under-covered corners of the United States and the world.

21. James Kinsella interview.

22. Paula Peters interview.

23. Mashpee Wampanoag Tribe website.

24. Conneller, 2019.

25. The original investors, operated under the name Trading Cove at Mashpee, were South African financiers, but violated *IGRA*. The Tribe terminated that agreement and subsequently Kien Huat (Genting Malaysia) became the main investor, financed the startups of Foxwoods Resort Casino in 1992 and the Seneca Niagara Casino in 2002 (Toensing, 2009).

26. Winkoor, 2020.

27. 2007 Senate Hearing 10-189.

28. S.1790 - National Defense Authorization Act for Fiscal Year 2020. Little Shell Tribe of Chippewa Indians Restoration Act of 2019.

29. \1\73 Fed. Reg. 30146-48 May 23, 2008.

30. Peterson, 2004.

31. Arlinda Locklear interview.

Chapter 11

Federal Recognition Does Not Equate to Casinos

> There are some who have suggested that tribal groups have petitioned for Federal recognition for the sole purpose of conducting gaming. However, if this were so, we would have to attribute to many of the petitioning tribal groups a clairvoyance that they knew that one day in the distant future there was going to be a Supreme Court decision and thereafter the Congress was going to enact a law authorizing and regulating the conduct of gaming, so they decided that they would file a letter of intent to begin the process of seeking Federal recognition.
> —Hon. Daniel K. Inouye, U.S. Senator from Hawaii[1]

The Seminole Tribe (Florida) built the first tribal casino in 1979.[2] Hollywood Seminole Bingo, a high-stakes bingo parlor opened in violation of the Florida Bingo Statute,[3] but eventually the Fifth Circuit Court of Appeals upheld a lower court ruling that the statute could not be enforced on the tribe's reservation. This opened the doors for other Tribes to consider bingo as an economic path often closed to Tribes because of centuries of broken treaties. Indian gaming is an entrepreneurial activity that enables Tribes to exercise their rights to create, develop, and sustain political, economic, and social systems.[4] In this way, they are not very different from other entrepreneurial activities that occur in the United States. However, gaming is one of the few economic resources available to Tribes that provide them with the income to revitalize their tribal traditions and sustain their cultures so that they can thrive into the future.[5] Moreover, entrepreneurial activities are not generally conducted for the collective good of a given community, as they are for Tribes, and it is not easy for a Tribe to open a gaming operation.

The crafters of the new federal recognition criteria completed in 2015 were cognizant of the false connection between federal recognition and gaming, and asserted that in the new rules, "Some think that the acknowledgment process is strongly related to gaming. The facts do not bear this out. Many of the petitioning groups came forward a long time ago."[6]

Since the first federal recognition criteria were established forty-three years ago, eighteen Tribes have been recognized. As of 2015, only eleven of the recognized Tribes had obtained land in trust, and only nine of those were currently engaged in gaming operations at that time.[7] It took an average of almost ten years after they received federal recognition for these nine Tribes to start these gaming enterprises. "The news media does not inform the public that the reason Tribes started petitions to become recognized is because trust lands along the Eastern seaboard (e.g., the Wampanoag) were being taken away from them, not to operate casinos," Paula Peters said.

Prior to the Supreme Court's Cabazon decision in 1987, gaming had not been an issue for Tribes that were going through the federal recognition process. Cabazon changed the trajectory for three Tribes that were in the process in the year leading up to the decision: the Alabama–Coushatta in Texas, and the Yselta del Sur Pueblo also in Texas, and the Wampanoag at Gay Head (Aquinnah Wampanoag) in Massachusetts.

Alabama–Coushatta had been terminated, so only Congress could restore its federal recognition. Since the government had never provided Yselta del Sur Pueblo services, and for other reasons, the two Tribes were restored together.[8] The Act was signed by President Ronald Reagan. Even though IGRA had yet to be passed, the legislative action allowing the restoration prohibited the Texas Tribes from engaging in gaming activities that were prohibited under Texas law, but also barred Texas from regulating gaming on those Tribes' lands. A number of lawsuits ensued that sought to legalize which body had regulatory jurisdiction over civil gaming: the state of Texas, or (in the case of the Wampanoag) the Commonwealth of Massachusetts. The Texas tribe's ability to game was eventually restored.[9] But the state of Texas continues to try to shut it down.[10] Shortly before this book went to print, the U.S. Supreme Court agreed to hear a case concerning whether and to what extent Texas could dictate what gaming is allowed at the Ysleta del Sur Pueblo.[11]

Other complications have arisen for the Aquinnah Wampanoag. In 1974, the Tribe filed a lawsuit against the Commonwealth of Massachusetts and the town of Gay Head about its title to certain aboriginal lands on the island of Martha's Vineyard. A 1983 settlement agreement allowed the transfer ownership of 485 acres of land in exchange for the tribe's release of claims on other aboriginal lands on Martha's Vineyard. The BIA approved the settlement, and Congress enacted legislation codifying the terms of the settlement agreement in 1987. In 2013, the National Indian Gaming Commission concluded that the 400 acres were eligible for tribal gaming under IGRA, and the Aquinnah said it would be starting construction on a Class II gaming facility. Then, in 2013, the Commonwealth of Massachusetts (later joined by the Town of Aquinnah and the Aquinnah/Gay Head Community Association) filed suit against the Tribe[12]; the federal trial court found in favor of the State, but the Tribe prevailed in U.S. Circuit Court of Appeals for the First Circuit, which concluded that the settlement lands were eligible for gaming under federal law and that the Tribe could move forward with its Class II gaming facility.[13] The opposed parties appealed the decision to the U.S. Supreme Court, which declined to consider the case. But when the case was remanded back down to the federal trial court, that court held that the Tribe still was required to abide by local zoning laws and acquire proper building permits, because the Tribe had not appealed that part of the trial court's decision—a holding that the First Circuit affirmed on appeal. Thirty-four years later, the Tribe still does not have a casino.

CABAZON'S EFFECT ON NEWS COVERAGE

> These attempts at acknowledgement were marching toward progress without a thought in [the Tribes] mind toward gaming. And then Cabazon happens. —Dan Lewerenz, NARF staff attorney and former NAJA president.[14]

News media coverage of the federal recognition of these three Tribes and their possible casinos was almost non-existent prior to the Cabazon decision. Only four news articles with the names of any of the three Tribes appeared prior to 1987 and three of the four were in Indigenous publications. None mentions gaming. The Boston Globe published the fourth.

Since January 1, 1987, 263 stories with the names of any of the three Tribes were published, and 202 of them refer to gaming. Arlinda Locklear agrees that the media are part of the problem of how federal recognition and casinos have become intertwined. But she also blames the process and government forces.

Federal recognition brings a Tribe closer to being eligible to operate a casino, but a rigorous standard must be met before a Tribe can start gaming. Even after a Tribe gains federal recognition, the Indian Gaming Regulatory Act must be consulted to decide if newly acquired trust land is eligible for a particular exemption or exception. Then a Tribe is required to go through a process in the Department of the Interior and the National Indian Gaming Commission to get the government to agree that the land is Indian land and eligible for gaming, which is time consuming and expensive.

There are numerous obstacles even after a Tribe becomes federally recognized before it can enter the gaming realm—or any kind of economic activity, including getting a parcel of land into trust which is governed under 25 CFR

Part 151.1 Locklear provided a scenario of the potential process to illustrate the level of complication. She has spent nearly fifty years in the practice of Native American law and is an expert on federal acknowledgment. She has defended Native American Tribes in federal and state claims related to treaty land and water rights, and to tribal jurisdiction on reservations with the Native American Rights Fund and Patton Boggs LLP. She was also the first licensed Native woman attorney to argue a case before the U.S. Supreme Court.

For example, Locklear said, a Tribe could submit the land to have it taken into trust and list the purpose as gaming; then the Department of the Interior's Office of Indian Gaming and solicitor's office gives the opinion. But, if a Tribe submits a gaming ordinance listing a specific parcel, then it goes to the NIGC for a decision. After that, the statute calls for additional processes. If a Tribe wants casino gaming (Class III) then the Tribe has to have a compact with the state where the land is located. If a Tribe has land and it wants a casino, then it has to be Indian Land. The definition of Indian Lands is either (a) Land within the limits of an Indian reservation; or (b) Land over which an Indian tribe exercises governmental power and that is either (1) Held in trust by the United States for the benefit of any Indian tribe or individual; or (2) Held by an Indian tribe or individual subject to restriction by the United States against alienation.[15] A Tribe must then petition the DOI to hold its land in trust, or if it doesn't have land but purchases it, a Tribe can ask the DOI to take the land as trust land under the Indian Reorganization Act. However, sometimes there is a specific mandatory statute for a particular Tribe that says they must take this land into trust, but mostly it's IRA. 25 CFR Part 151 lays out the trust acquisition process under the IRA. To get land taken into trust under the IRA, under one of the definitions of Indian, Tribes had to have been under federal jurisdiction when the IRA was enacted in 1934.[16]

If the land is to be used for developmental purposes (such as for a casino), then the process is even more complicated. In addition to the cost of acquiring the land, it requires an Environmental Impact Statement (EIS), which ranges from $60,000 to a high of $85 million[17] and takes an average of 3.5 years;[18] however, it can take longer if the Tribe is sued. There is also the administrative process for getting it into trust, which is a multistep process for things like hotels and golf courses[19] and a different process for gaming operations. This can cost from $500,000 to $1 million and can take another couple of years to get the land actually into trust.

Meanwhile, there is a separate set of laws and regulations to determine whether or not the land is actually eligible for gaming. A provision in the 1988 Gaming Regulatory Act says, "land acquired in trust after the enactment of this Statute is not eligible unless it meets one of four exceptions."

Until a Tribe has its own territory either held in trust or created in Indian Country, it is difficult to establish itself as a truly self-determining Native community. The IRA, which authorizes the Secretary of the Interior to acquire land for a Tribe, does not include money for the Secretary to purchase land for Tribes. Therefore, if Tribes are going to get tribal territory, they have to purchase that land themselves. Nonfederally recognized Tribes have to find someone to finance their purchase, and that is usually the gaming industry.

Locklear succinctly described the complicated, years-long process: "First you have to get the land, then you have to get the EIS, then you've got to get it placed into trust, and then you have to get the Secretary of the Interior to determine if that land is gaming eligible if it was acquired in trust after 1988." A Tribe will then need to hire gaming lawyers if it wants a casino. For Class III gaming, it needs a compact with the state. Class II gaming (which consists of bingo and related games, including electronic versions of those games) can take place without a compact under IGRA, but other laws and regulations need to be followed. "Either way, it takes at least another year. And inevitably, someone will sue to stop the gaming. Often this is someone in Las Vegas."

NOTES

1. S. Hrg 109–91 at 3.
2. Indian Gaming, Brittanica.com accessed October 27, 2021.
3. *Seminole Tribe of Florida v. Butterworth*, 658 F.2d 310 (5th Cir. 1981) affirmed the district court's finding that the Florida bingo statute "was regulatory in nature and therefore could not be enforced against the [Seminole] tribe."
4. Colbourne, 2017.
5. Dana, 2007.
6. 25 CFR § 83, p. 37864.
7. Department of the Interior, 2015. Acknowledged and denied petitions and those decided by Congressional Action are listed on the DOI website here https://www.bia.gov/as-ia/ofa/decided-cases.
8. Ysleta del Sur Pueblo and Alabama and Coushatta Indian Tribe of Texas Restoration Act Pub. L. No. 100-89, 101 Stat. 666.
9. H. Rept. 116-165 - Ysleta del Sur Pueblo and Alabama-Coushatta Tribe of Texas equal and fair opportunity settlement act.
10. Conneller, 2019.
11. *Ysleta del Sur Pueblo v. Texas*, No. 20-493 (petition granted October 18, 2021).
12. The Wampanoag Tribe and Massachusetts signed a Memorandum of Understanding in November 1983 which conveyed the Settlement Lands—consisting of approximately 485 acres—to the Tribe. *Massachusetts v. Wampanoag Tribe of Gay Head (Aquinnah)*, 853 F.3d 618, 622 (1st Cir. 2017) (*Wampanoag I*). Congress implemented the Settlement Agreement by passing the Wampanoag Tribal Council of Gay Head, Inc., Indian Claims Settlement Act on August 18, 1987. *Id.* In May 2013,

the Tribe submitted an amended Gaming Ordinance stating their intention to pursue Class II gaming—this was approved by the NIGC in October 2013 under IGRA. *Id.* at 623. The NIGC stated that the Settlement Lands (approx. 485 acres) were eligible for gaming under IGRA. *Id.* Massachusetts filed suit on December 2, 2013. *Id.* The First Circuit held that "the Tribe ha[d] exercised more than sufficient governmental power to satisfy the requirements of the IGRA" and therefore the IGRA did apply to their Settlement Lands. *Id.* at 621.

13. "Class II gaming is defined as the game of chance commonly known as bingo (which may include the use of electronic, computer, or other technological aids) and if played in the same location as the bingo, pull tabs, punch boards, tip jars, instant bingo, and other games similar to bingo. Class II gaming also includes non-banked card games, that is, games that are played exclusively against other players rather than the house or a player acting as a bank." National Indian Gaming Association website https://www.nigc.gov/commission/history. Accessed May 20, 2021.

14. Dan Lewerenz interview.

15. 25 CFR § 502.12.

16. "[F]or purposes of § 479, the phrase "now under Federal jurisdiction" refers to a tribe that was under federal jurisdiction at the time of the statute's enactment. As a result, § 479 limits the Secretary's authority to taking land into trust for the purpose of providing land to members of a tribe that was under federal jurisdiction when the IRA was enacted in June 1934." *Carcieri v. Salazar*, 555 U.S. 379, 382 (2009).

17. United States Government Accountability Office, 2014.

18. DeWitt & DeWitt, 2008.

19. Department of the Interior, 2014.

Chapter 12

Indigenous Standpoint Journalism for Non-Indigenous Journalists

If journalists truly want to inform their audiences about what federal recognition means to their communities, they need to rethink how they have covered it in the past. "The news media don't have a historical perspective on federal recognition, and they don't understand why non-federally recognized Tribes exist, and why the issue has nothing to do with gaming at all," Arlinda Locklear said. Paula Peters added that journalists need to understand that federal recognition is a tool, and not always the best tool. However, it's hard for mainstream journalists to understand this. Any diversity in a newsroom is good, she said. "But having Indigenous people in the newsroom that can inform other journalists changes the story."

But very few Indigenous journalists work in mainstream media, and even fewer are leaders. Leadership must change if more progress is to be made. If mainstream newsrooms can learn to cover their communities from the perspective of their communities, then the paradigm shifts, and the United States truly has a news media that covers all of America. It is suggested that journalists think about Indigenous Standpoint Theory as a way to cover federal recognition, so that it covers it in a way that disseminates knowledge, doesn't ignore the communities it affects, and doesn't have devastating consequences for Tribes and Indigenous people.

IMPLEMENTING INDIGENOUS STANDPOINT THEORY

Academic research on news coverage of Indigenous communities often uses traditional western theories that legitimize knowledge about these communities from a non-Indigenous perspective. The mainstream news coverage analyzed in this book also uses non-Indigenous storytelling. Therefore, just as that academic knowledge becomes the dominant academic literature upon which future research relies, the journalism becomes the dominant story in which policymakers and the public understand Tribes. That journalism all too often ignores, erases, and co-opts the knowledge that Indigenous journalists inherently understand about their own communities, and the ways the communities have developed over time to collect and disseminate knowledge. Indigenous journalism is a purposeful act of reclaiming that knowledge to benefit Indigenous communities instead of considering Indigenous communities as deficient. "For decades, research on Indigenous peoples, people of color, marginalized people, has been very deficit oriented, it's been damaging, harmful, exploitative. And in order to decolonize, [researchers] have to consciously move away from those approaches"[1] and be proactively in support of Indigenous peoples. The news media industry needs to adopt this perspective also.

Journalists should strive to fairly and accurately report on Indigenous people and Indigenous communities. The Society of Professional Journalists Code of Ethics asks journalists to "Boldly tell the story of diversity and the magnitude of the human experience. Seek sources whose voices we rarely hear, and avoid stereotyping."[2] This starts by knowing the history and politics of the people whose land they occupy. The 2021 Native American Journalists Association (NAJA) Media *Spotlight Report*[3] found more than half of the 300 *New York Times* articles published between 2015 and 2021 used stereotypes found on the NAJA Bingo Card.

In addition to the excellent advice offered by the NAJA's Reporting Guides (NAJA.com), it is recommended journalists do the following:

- Understand the politics of Indigenous people and what they have survived, and how they have remained resilient.
- Strive to understand what controversies between Tribes really mean, and why other Tribes might block another tribe's pursuit of federal recognition.
- Build and sustain relationships with tribal leaders, elders, community members, particularly women and Indigenous government officials.
- Work proactively in support of Indigenous peoples by understanding their issues instead of just covering them.
- Understand the power of storytelling in Indian Country, and how those stories can inform non-Indigenous readers to provide a more accurate picture.
- Collaborate on news coverage with Indigenous journalists.
- Provide opportunities and welcoming spaces for Indigenous peoples to engage with reporters and news organizations.
- Add Indigenous journalists to editorial boards and hire them in newsrooms and pay them the same wages as non-Indigenous journalists.

- Support organizations such as NAJA by attending its conferences, supporting its efforts, and utilizing its many resources.
- Incorporating training from NAJA into professional development opportunities.
- Publish stories from Indigenous news outlets on non-Native platforms.
- Learn how local tribal governments operate, and the history of the Tribes.
- Cover the issues facing nonfederally recognized Tribes, whether they are state recognized or not.
- Recognize that gaming is both a tool and a right and so strive to include historical frames in stories.
- Know that Tribes existed for centuries before gaming was considered a path to economic independence for Tribes, and hopefully they will exist for centuries more, with or without them.
- Look at the history of gaming in tribal communities even before casinos and bingo. Gaming was part of many tribal cultures prior to using them as an economic resource.

The final advice is the advice that the grandmother of Indigenous theories and methodologies gives academic researchers, "Look with love and joy and see the good and then ask the question." —Linda Smith Tuhiwai.[4]

NOTES

1. Smith, 2021.
2. For the full code see https://www.spj.org/ethicscode.asp.
3. 2021 NAJA Media *Spotlight Report,* https://najanewsroom.com/2021-naja-media-spotlight-report/.
4. Smith, 2021.

Epilogue

A Final Story About Federal Recognition and COVID-19 and Casinos

The COVID-19 epidemic that began in 2020 disproportionately affected Indigenous people and other people of color.[1] Tribes without federal recognition were left struggling to help their members due to inadequate resources that might have mitigated the effects of the pandemic on their members who were already suffering from health conditions (e.g., heart disease, lung disease, asthma, diabetes, kidney disease, liver disease, and autoimmune diseases). Indigenous people are at higher risk for severe COVID-19 illness and death.[2] The social distancing needed to stop the spread of COVID-19 has posed a huge hurdle, as 10 percent of Indigenous people age fifty and older live in multigenerational households, compared to 6.5 percent in the general U.S. population. This close-knit living arrangement is driven in part by tribal cultures that emphasize community and multigenerational living.[3]

Although the 574 federally recognized Tribes are at risk from the same health disparities as non-recognized Tribes, they received a collective $8 billion from the Coronavirus Aid, Relief, and Economic Security Act approved in March 2020.[4] The Tribes used the funds for such necessities as food, personal protective equipment, sanitation supplies, COVID-19 testing, business support, housing relief, education, and vaccination efforts.[5] Tribes also received priority for COVID-19 tests and vaccines. By March 2021, the Indian Health Service (IHS) had administered one million COVID-19 vaccine doses (accounting for 60 percent of IHS users). According to a Wall Street Journal analysis of CDC data, among U.S. counties of 1,000 people or more, 12 of the 15 counties with the highest vaccination rates in the country were on Indian reservations or in Alaska Native communities, where the IHS or tribal health clinics are a primary source of care.[6] By April 2021, federal data showed that 32 percent of American Indian and Alaska Native people had received at least one vaccine dose compared to 19 percent of White people, 16 percent of Asian Americans, 12 percent of African Americans, and 9 percent of Latinos.[7]

To subsidize the always under-funded IHS, Indigenous-run industries provide support and sustain tribal communities and their members through the collective efforts of those industries. Gaming operations are one of the few viable economic resources available for Native Nations to alleviate these disparities,[8] although it has been accused of taking a "social toll"[9] on communities in an aggregate, which ignores the unique relationship of tribal communities and casinos.[10] Tribal gaming operations were a critical economic resource in Indian Country that was lost consequent to pervasive business closures resulting from the COVID-19 pandemic in the spring of 2020.[11] "Tribal governments use gaming revenue to fund social service programs, including scholarships, health-care clinics, substance abuse programs, education, law enforcement, and tribal courts."[12]

Many tribal gaming operations closed their doors over the concern of spreading COVID-19, including 14 in New Mexico[13] and 130 in Oklahoma at the beginning of the pandemic.[14] All tribal casinos (and many non-gaming tribal businesses) had closed by April 2020[15] leaving Tribes without the sources of revenue they depend on to pay for expenses related to health, education, and economic development, and, generally, to support the basic needs of their communities as well as tribal infrastructure.[16]

Research shows Tribes with casinos are able to increase economic activity, lower unemployment, and achieve better health and lower mortality rates for their members.[17] However, only federally recognized Tribes have the option to engage in gaming businesses. A future study should examine whether Tribes with gaming operations had better COVID-19 mitigation financial resources than Tribes without them.

Access to funds that come with federal recognition provide protection for individual members of the Tribe, and—wrapped into that—is the protection of tribal cultures by ensuring survival of tribal elders. Tribal elders pass on language and culture of the Tribe; their loss could mean irreversible loss of that knowledge to be passed on to future generations. But the retention of cultural knowledge takes money. Federal recognition ensures that Tribes have access to specific funds, but many state and U.S. government strings are attached to these funds. Combining gaming revenue with these funds provides Tribes with some modicum of economic empowerment—despite the fact that Tribes and their members have been subject to genocide and white supremacy for more than 400 years—enabling tribal members to have a chance to be the resilient cultures they have always been.

NOTES

1. Marshall, 2020.
2. Fernando, 2021; HSS.gov.
3. Pindus et al., 2017.
4. U.S. Department of the Interior, BIA.gov.
5. Fernando, 2021.
6. Whelan, 2021.
7. Hill & Artiga, 2021; Whelan, 2021.
8. Azocar et al, 2021.
9. Goldin, 1999, p. 835.
10. Gorin, 1999.
11. See Azocar et al., 2021.
12. National Congress of American Indians, 2020a, para. 2.
13. NewMexico.gov, 2020.
14. Mills, 2020.
15. Harvard Project on American Indian Economic Development, 2020.
16. IGRA; Smith, 2020.
17. Evans & Topeleski, 2002.

Appendix A
Broadcast News Sources Indexed by Lexis Nexis

The database searched contains all available news transcripts from the following sources. International sources were excluded.

American Public Media
BC News Transcripts
Bloomberg: *For The Record*
Bloomberg: *On the Economy with Tom Keene*
Bloomberg: *Political Capital with Al Hunt*
Bloomberg: *Surveillance Midday*
Bloomberg: *Surveillance Show*
Bloomberg: *TV*
Bloomberg: *Venture*
Business Day TV—Transcripts
Cavuto
CBS News Transcripts
The Charlie Rose Show
CNBC/Dow Jones Business Video
CNN
CNN *Financial All*
CNN International
CQ Congressional Testimony
CQ Transcriptions
CQ Transcriptions (Hearings)
Dan Rather Reports
Embedded
ET Now Transcripts
FD (Fair Disclosure) Wire
FDCH News Service Capitol Report
Federal News Service
Federal News Service—Hearings
Financial Market Regulatory Wire
Follow The Money

Foreign Correspondent
Fox Business *Happy Hour*
Fox News Network
Freedom Watch
Global Broadcast Database—English (Full Text)
How I Built This
Imus Simulcast
Intelligence Report
The Kennedy Show
Lou Dobbs Tonight
Money for Breakfast
The Montel Williams Show
Mornings With Maria
MSNBC
NBC News
The Nightly Business Report
NPR *All Things Considered*
NPR *Code Switch* (North America)
NPR *Fresh Air*
NPR *Hidden Brain*
NPR *Morning Edition*
NPR National Public Radio Archive
NPR *Planet Money*
NPR *TED Radio Hour*
NPR *Wait Wait Don't Tell Me!*
NPR *Weekend All Things Considered*
NPR *Weekend Edition Saturday*
NPR *Weekend Edition Sunday*
PBS NewsHour (formerly *The NewsHour with Jim Lehrer*)
Power and Money
Presidential Campaign Press Materials
Risk & Reward (Fox)
SEC Wire
Stossel

Appendix B
Magazines Indexed by ProQuest

1. *Crain's Chicago Business*; Chicago, Illinois
2. *D*; Dallas, Texas
3. *Diablo Business: DB*; Walnut Creek, California
4. *Florida Trend*; St. Petersburg, Florida
5. *Hispanic*; Miami
6. *Los Angeles Magazine*; Los Angeles, California
7. *Louisville Magazine Inc. Louisville*; Louisville, Kentucky
8. *Meet the Press*; Washington D.C.
9. *MSP Communications St. Paul*; Minneapolis, Minnesota
10. *New Jersey Business*; Newark, New Jersey
11. *New Mexico Business Journal*; Albuquerque, New Mexico
12. *New Orleans Magazine*; New Orleans, Louisiana
13. *New York Times Book Review*; New York, New York
14. *New York Times Magazine*; New York, New York
15. *The Public Record*; Palm Desert, California
16. *Regardie's*; Washington D.C.
17. *St. Louis Commerce Magazine*; St. Louis, Missouri
18. *Texas Monthly*; Austin, Texas
19. *Vermont Business Magazine*; Brattleboro, Vermont
20. *The Weekly Standard*; Washington D.C.
21. *Western New York*; Buffalo New York
22. *WSJ: the Magazine from the Wall Street Journal*; New York, New York

Appendix C
U.S. Indigenous News Sources Indexed by Ethnic News Watch

TITLE	Publisher	Publication	Full Text
News from Native California	News from Native California	Berkeley, Calif.	Sep. 30, 1996
Char-Koosta News	Char-Koosta News	Pablo, Mont.	Oct. 11, 1991
Fort Apache Scout	White Mountain Apache Tribe	Whiteriver, Ariz.	April 30, 1964
The Circle: News from an American Indian Perspective	Minneapolis American Indian Center	Minneapolis, Minn.	March 1, 1994
Cherokee Advocate	Cherokee Nation		Feb. 26, 1977
Cherokee Observer	Cherokee Nation	Parkhill, Okla.	Jan. 31, 1994
Cherokee Phoenix	Cherokee Nation	Tahlequah, Okla.	Feb. 29, 1992
The Native Nevadan	Reno Sparks Tribal Council	Reno, Nev.	Oct. 31, 1991
Navajo Times	Navajo Times	Window Rock, Ariz.	Feb. 8, 1995
News From Indian Country	Indian Country Communications	Hayward, Wis.	March 31, 1985
North American Post	North American Post Publishing, Inc.	Seattle, Wash.	May 16, 1997
Ojibwe Akiing	Indian Country Communications	Hayward, Wis.	Dec. 31, 1996
Red Sticks Press	Red Sticks Press	St. Petersburg, Fla.	June 30, 1994
Seminole Tribune	Seminole Tribune	Hollywood, Fla.	March 2, 1984
Sho-Ban News	Fort Hall Business Council	Fort Hall, Idaho	Jan. 3, 1979
Tundra Times	Eskimo Indian Aleut Publishing Company	Anchorage, Alaska	June 16, 1993
The Cherokee Voice	Georgia Southern University	Statesboro, Georgia	June 30, 1999
Native American Times	Native American Times	Tulsa, Okla.	Feb. 29, 2000

TITLE	Publisher	Publication	Full Text
O'odham Action News	Salt River Pima-Maricopa Tribe	Scottsdale, Ariz.	April 1, 1994
Wind River News	Wind River News	Lander, Wyo.	Dec. 25, 1984
Country Road Chronicles	Country Road Chronicles	Dingman's Ferry, Penn.	Sept. 4, 1997
Indian Country Today	Indian Country Today	Oneida, N.Y.	April 14, 1983
The Native Voice	Native Voice Publishing	Rapid City, S.D.	March 28, 2002
The Navajo Nation Today	Navajo Nation Today	Window Rock, Ariz.	Oct. 15, 1991
Northwest Nikkei	North American Post Publishing, Inc.	Seattle, Wash.	April 1, 1994
The Ojibwe News	Native American Press, Ojibwe News	St. Paul, Minn.	Jan. 7, 1994
Pequot Times	Mashantucket Pequot Tribal Nation	Mashantucket, Conn.	Jan. 31, 2000

Appendix D

List of the Mainstream Broadcast Stories that Included References to Federal Recognition

"Urban Rez" Explores What It Means To Be Native American
NPR Weekend *All Things Considered*|Apr. 30, 2016|689

A Nation of Freeloaders?
Stossel|Jul. 05, 2012|NEWS; Financial|6758|John Stossel

5 *KFVE* Honolulu, HI
Global Broadcast Database - English (Full Text)|May 03, 2010|631

As Requirements Change, Just Who Is An Indian?
NPR *Morning Edition*|May 11, 2009|1229

Lumbees' Tribal Recognition Depends on Senate
NPR *All Things Considered*|Jul. 18, 2007|907

C-SPAN
Global Broadcast Database - English (Full Text)|Jun. 07, 2007|650

Virginia's Monacan Indian Nation Seeks Recognition
NPR Weekend *All Things Considered*|Mar. 25, 2007|2068

For the Wampanoag, Wait for Recognition Is Over
NPR National Public Radio Archive|Apr. 18, 2006|605

Hawaiian Sovereignty
NPR National Public Radio Archive|Jul. 25, 2005|5404

Haunani Apoliona Discusses a Bill That Would Grant Native Hawaiians the Same Legal Status as Many Native American Tribes
NPR National Public Radio Archive|Jul. 20, 2005|796

Native American Identity
NPR National Public Radio Archive|Sep. 20, 2004|8219

Smithsonian National Museum of the American Indian
NPR National Public Radio Archive|Sep. 20, 2004|7406

Beverly Wright and Russell Means Discuss Issues That Plague Tribal Communities
NPR National Public Radio Archive|Nov. 26, 2003|Interview|1374

Al Gore Won't Seek President in 2004; New York Transit Strike Averted
CNN Transcripts|Dec. 16, 2002|News; Domestic; SHOW|7678|Aaron Brown, Robert Novak, Jonathan Karl, Jeanne Meserve, Bob Franken

Effort of the Schaghticoke Tribal Nation as They Seek Federal Recognition from the Bureau of Indian Affairs
NPR *All Things Considered*|Oct. 29, 2002|2208

Wampum Wonderland; Legitimacy of Casinos Run by Indians
CBS News Transcripts|May 23, 2000|Profile|2575

Native American Museum
NPR *Morning Edition*|Aug. 11, 1998|News; Domestic; correction|1207|Tandaleya Wilder, Stamford; Bob Edwards, Washington, D.C.

Nativeness
NPR *All Things Considered*|Jul. 20, 1998|News; Domestic; PACKAGE|1559|Leda Hartman; Linda Wertheimer, Washington, D.C.; Noah Adams

Native American Sovereignty
NPR National Public Radio Archive|May 14, 1998|News; Domestic; FEATURE|7911|Ray Suarez, Salt Lake City

The Invisible People, Part 7—Identity Crisis
CNN Transcripts|Oct. 30, 1994|News; Domestic; Package|1195

Wappo Indians Ask Government for Official Recognition
CNN Transcripts|Apr. 17, 1994|News; Domestic; Package|400|SUSAN REED

Your Land Is My Land
ABC News Transcripts|Aug. 13, 1993|News; Domestic; Show; Show|7808

Appendix E

Questions Posed to Lee Fleming, Director of the Office of Acknowledgment

1. Once a completed petition reaches your office, what is the step-by-step process and who is involved in that process?
2. Are the Tribes that were in process before the new criteria was in place going through the new criteria? Or, can they choose to go through the old one?
3. It doesn't seem that any Tribes have been recognized under the updated 2015 process, is that correct?
4. How does the Interior Board of Indian Appeals review petitions that receive a negative decision? Where can I find information about who is on the board and how they become board members?
5. If a Tribe doesn't have the funds needed to fund the recognition process, are there resources to help them?
6. I've learned that petitions were fairly short when they first started after 1979. What changed to make them so long? Is there any documentation or data about the average length of petitions?
7. Does the OFA have a conflict-of-interest policy?
8. Is there a list that shows which federally recognized Tribes went through the administrative process and those that went through the legislative process? And/or is there a list that shows the legislatively recognized Tribes that had to give up gaming prospects?
9. Is there an exhaustive list that shows the dates that Tribes received federal recognition (including when they started)?

10. What is the length of time a Tribe that goes through the new process can expect to receive a decision once it has filed a completed petition?
11. Are the people involved in the OFA appointed? Is there a list of the staff and their credentials and how long they've worked there? Who hires the staff that oversees the petitions?
12. Are there questions that journalists should ask of the OFA when reporting on Tribes going through the acknowledgment process?

Bibliography

1926 supplement to the Virginia code of 1924; containing all the general laws of 1926 with full annotations. (1926). Charlottesville: The Michie Company.

Adams, Kenneth. Interviewed by Azocar, Cristina. Personal interview on February 11, 2021.

Adams, Mikaela A. *Who Belongs? Race, Resources, and Tribal Citizenship in the Native South*. New York, NY: Oxford University Press. (2016), 32.

American Society of News Editors Annual Census, "Minority Percentages at Participating Organizations." (2018). https://www.asne.org/diversity-survey-percent

Ardill, Arlan A. "Australian Sovereignty, Indigenous Standpoint Theory and Feminist Standpoint Theory: First Peoples' Sovereignties Matter." *Griffith Law Review*, 22(2) (January, 2013), 315–343.

Ashley, Laura and Beth Olson. "Constructing Reality: Print Media's Framing of the Women's Movement, 1966 to 1986." *Journalism & Mass Communication Quarterly*, 75(2) (1998), 263–277.

Azocar, Cristina L. *The Reading Red Report 2007: A Content Analysis of General Audience Newspapers in Circulation Areas with High Percentages of Native Americans. A NewsWatch Project Report*. San Francisco, CA: Center for Integration and Improvement of Journalism. (2007).

Azocar, Cristina L., LaPoe, Victoria, Olson, Candi Carter, LaPoe, Benjamin and Hazarika, Bharlbi. "Indigenous Communities and COVID-19: Reporting on Resources and Resilience." *Howard Journal of Communications* (2013). DOI: 10.1080/10646175.2021.1892552.

Backhouse, Paul. "A Big Year for the People Made From the Sands of Florida." *Seminole Tribune*, January 31, 2017. http://jpllnet.sfsu.edu/login?url=https://www-proquest-com.jpllnet.sfsu.edu/newspapers/big-year-people-made-sands-florida/docview/1869920051/se-2?accountid=13802.

Battiste, Marie. "Enabling the Autumn Seed: Toward a Decolonized Approach Toward Aboriginal Knowledge, Language and Education." *Canadian Journal of Native Education,* 22(1) (1998), 16–27.

Berkhofer, Jr., Robert F. *The White Man's Indian: Images of the American Indian from Columbus to the Present.* New York, NY: Vintage Books. (1978).

Booker, Betty. "Indian Leader in State Dies—Thomasina Jordan Was Rights Activist." *Richmond Times-Dispatch.* (May 25, 1999. B1).

Borona, Kendi. "Reclaiming Indigenous Knowledge Systems." In *Reclaiming Indigenous Knowledge Systems.* Newcastle-upon-Tyne: Cambridge Scholars Publisher. (2019).

Brewer, Marilyn B. and Kathleen P. Pierce. "Social Identity Complexity and Outgroup Tolerance." *Personality and Social Psychology Bulletin,* 31(1) (March, 2005), 428–437. doi:10.1177/0146167204271710.

Briggs, Kara. *Reading Red Report.* Native American Journalists Association. Vermillion, SD. (2003).

Brown, Aaron. "Newsnight." CNN. (December 16, 2002).

Brown, Alleen. "Five Spills, Six Months in Operation: Dakota Access Track Record Highlights Unavoidable Reality—Pipelines Leak." *The Intercept.* (January 9, 2018).

Bruck, Peter A. "Strategies for Peace, Strategies for News Research." *Journal of Communication,* 39 (March 1989), 108–129.

Burton, Greg. Interviewed by Azocar, Cristina on February 25, 2021.

Bush on Native American Issues: "Tribal Sovereignty Means That. It's Sovereign." *Democracy Now!* (August, 2004). Retrieved at https://archive.org/details/dn2004-0810_vid.

Cama, Timothy. "Dakota Access Pipeline Now in Service." *The Hill.* (June 1, 2017).

Carragee, Kevin M. *News and Ideology: an Analysis of Coverage of the West German Green Party by the New York Times.* Columbia, S.C: Association for Education in Journalism and Mass Communication, 1991.

Carstarphen, Meta G. and John P. Sanchez, J. P. (Eds.). *American Indians and the Mass Media.* ProQuest Ebook Central (2012).

Choy, Sarojni and Julie Woodlock, "Implementing Indigenous Standpoint Theory: Challenges for a TAFE Trainer." *International Journal of Training Research,* 5(1), (April, 2007), 39–54.

Colbourne, Rick. "An Understanding of Native American Entrepreneurship." *Small Enterprise Research,* 24(1) (2017), 49–61. https://doi.org/10.1080/13215906.2017.1289856.

Coleman, Arica L. *That the Blood Stay Pure: African Americans, Native Americans, and the Predicament of Race and Identity in Virginia.* Bloomington, IN: Indiana University Press. (2013).

Collier, John. Memorandum, Hearing on H.R. 7902 before the House Committee on Indian Affairs. 73rd Cong., 2d Sess., (1934), 16–18.

Collins, Patricia. "Comment on Hekman's 'Truth and Method: Feminist Standpoint Theory Revisited': Where's the Power?" *Signs* (1997), 375.

Condon, Tom. "Time for Feds to Recognize the Harm of Casino Tribes." *Hartford Courant* [State Edition] Feb. 8, 2004. Retrieved from https://search-proquest-com.jpllnet.sfsu.edu/docview/256741824?accountid=13802.

Conneller, Philip. "El Paso's Tigua Pueblo Tribe Ordered to Shutter Speaking Rock Casino, Ops Ruled Illegal Under Texas Law." *Casino.org* (February 19, 2019). https://www.casino.org/news/tigua-pueblo-tribe-ordered-to-shutter-speaking-rock-casino/.

Conneller, Phillip. "Genting Cuts Financial Support for Distressed Mashpee Wampanoag Tribe." *Casino.org*. (March 4, 2019). https://www.casino.org/news/genting-cuts-financial-support-for-distressed-mashpee-wampanoag-tribe/.

Cook, Samuel R. "The Monacan Indian Nation: Asserting Tribal Sovereignty in the Absence of Federal Recognition." *Wicazo Sa Review*, 17(2), (2002), 91–116. https://doi.org/10.1353/wic.2002.0016.

Copeland, David A. *Colonial American Newspapers: Character and Content*. Newark, NJ: University of Delaware Press. (1977).

Coward, John M. *The Newspaper Indian: Native American Identity in the Press, 1820–1890*. Urbana, IL: University of Illinois Press. (1999).

Cramer, Renee Ann. *Cash, Color and Colonialism: The Politics of Tribal Acknowledgment*. Norman, OK: University of Oklahoma Press. (2005).

Cushman, Ellen. *The Cherokee Syllabary: Writing the People's Perseverance*. University of Oklahoma Press (2011).

Cutlip, Kimbra. "In 1868, Two Nations Made a Treaty, the U.S. Broke It and Plains Indian Tribes are Still Seeking Justice." *Smithsonian Magazine* (November 7, 2018). Accessed Feb. 24, 2021 https://www.smithsonianmag.com/smithsonian-institution/1868-two-nations-made-treaty-us-broke-it-and-plains-indian-tribe-are-still-seeking-justice-180970741/.

Dana, Leo Paul. "Toward a Multidisciplinary Definition of Indigenous Entrepreneurship." In Dana, Leo Paul and Robert Brent, Anderson (Eds.), *International Handbook of Research on Indigenous Entrepreneurship*. Cheltenham: Edward Elgar (2007), 3–7.

Daniels, George L. "The Role of Native American Print and Online Media in the 'Era of Big Stories': A Comparative Case Study of Native American Outlets,' Coverage of the Red Lake Shootings." *Journalism*, 7(3), (2006), 321–242.

Definition of Indian Lands, U.S. Code 502.12 (1992), 25 CFR § 502.12.

Deal, Jodi. "Pamunkey Tribe Hits Milestone in Recognition." *Richmond Times-Dispatch*. (Feb. 4, 2014). Retrieved at http://www.richmond.com/news/local/hanover/mechanicsville-local/pamunkey-tribe-hits-milestone-in-recognition/article_444e907a-8dc7-11e3-a434-001a4bcf6878.html.

Deloria, Phillip J. *Playing Indian*. New Haven, CT: Yale University Press. (1998).

Deloria, Vine. *Custer Died for Your Sins*. Norman, OK: Oklahoma University Press. (1998).

Department of the Interior. Bureau of Indian Affairs. "Indian Entities Recognized By and Eligible to Receive Services from the Bureau of Indian Affairs." *Federal Register* 86(18) (2021), 7554–7558.

Department of the Interior. "Fee-to-Trust Quick Reference Guide Release #13-90, Version III" (rev 4), Issued June 16, 2014.

DeWitt, Piet and Carole A. DeWitt. "How Long Does it Take to Prepare an Environmental Impact Statement?" *Environmental Practice*, 10(4), (2009), 164–174. doi:10.1017/S146604660808037X.

Dippie, Brian W. *The Vanishing American: White Attitudes and U.S. Indian Policy.* Lawrence, KS: University of Kansas Press. (1982).

Diver, Sibyl. "Negotiating Indigenous Knowledge at the Science-Policy Interface: Insights from the Xáxli'p Community Forest." *Environmental Science & Policy,* 73 (July, 2017), 1–11. https://doi.org/10.1016/j.envsci.2017.03.001

DOI, former staff member interview March 16, 2021.

Downs, Hugh and Barbara Walters. "Your Land Is My Land," ABC News *20/20.* (August 13, 1993).

Dunbar-Ortiz, Roxanne and Dina Gilio-Whitaker, D. *"All the Real Indians Died Off": And 20 Other Myths About Native Americans.* Boston, MA: Beacon Press (2016).

Dussias, Allison M. "Protecting Pocahontas' World: The Mattaponi Tribe's Struggle Against Virginia's King William Reservoir Project." *American Indian Law Review,* 36(1) (2011), 1–123.

Edelman, Murray. *Constructing the Political Spectacle.* Chicago: University of Chicago Press. (1998).

Edington, John M. *Indigenous Environmental Knowledge Reappraisal.* Springer International Publishing AG. (2017). https://doi.org/10.1007/978-3-319-62491-4

Entman, Robert M. "Framing: Toward Clarification of a Fractured Paradigm." *Journal of Communication,* 43(4) (December, 1993), 51–58.

Estrada, Vivian M. "The Tree of Life as a Research Methodology." *Australian Journal of Indigenous Education,* 34 (January 2005), 44–52.

Evans, William N. and Julie Topoleski. "The Social and Economic Impacts of Native American Casinos." NBER Working Papers Number 9198. (September 2002).

Fawzi, Nayla. "Beyond Policy Agenda-Setting: Political Actors' and Journalists' Perceptions of News Media Influence Across All Stages of the Political Process." *Information, Communication & Society,* 21(8) (August 2016), 1134–1150. doi:10.1080/1369118X.2017.1301524

Federally Recognized Indian Tribe List Act of 1994, U.S. Code 108 Stat. §§4791, 4792.

Federated Indians of Graton Rancheria. "A Restored Tribe Serving Marin and Sonoma Counties." Website accessed February 15, 2021. https://gratonrancheria.com/

Fenelon, Jams V. *Culturicide, Resistance, and Survival of the Lakota (Sioux Nation).* New York, NY: Routledge. (2014).

Fernando, Christina. "Pandemic Leaves Tribes Without U.S. Recognition at Higher Risk." *Associated Press.* (February 27, 2021). Retrieved from https://abcnews.go.com/Health/wireStory/pandemic-leaves-tribe-us-recognition-higher-risk-76153872.

Finkelman, Paul and Tim Alan Garrison (Eds.). *Encyclopedia of United States Indian Policy and Law.* Washington, DC: Sage. (2009).

Fixico, Donald L. "Indian-White Relations in the United States, 1900 to the Present." In Frederick E. Hoxie (Ed.), *Encyclopedia of North American Indians.* Boston, MA: Houghton Mifflin. (1996).

Foley, Dennis. "Indigenous Epistemology and Indigenous Standpoint Theory." *Social Alternatives,* 22(1), (2003), 44–52.

Forbes, Jack. D. "The Manipulation of Race, Caste, and Identity: Classifying Afro Americans, Native Americans and Red-Black People." *Journal of Ethnic Studies*, 17(4) (1990), 1–51.

Forbes, Jack D. "Blood Quantum: A Relic of Racism and Termination." *Native Intelligence from The People's Voice*. (2000). Retrieved from http://www.weyanoke.org/reading/jdf-BloodQuantum.html.

Fremlin, Jenny. "Agenda Setting: Independent vs. Corporate Media." *Journal of New Communications Research*, 3(1), (2008), 55–64.

Frazier, Stephen. "The Invisible People, Part 7—Identity Crisis." CNN News (Oct./30, 1994).

Furshong, Gabriel. "Will the Little Shell Tribe Finally be Recognized?" *Char-Koosta News*. (Feb. 4, 2016).

Gamson, William A. *Talking Politics*. Cambridge: Cambridge University Press. (1992).

Getches, David H., Charles F. Wilkinson, and Robert L. Williams. *Cases and Materials on Federal Indian Law*. St. Paul, MN: Thomson/West. (2005).

Gilroy, John, Donnelly, Michelle, Colmar, Susan, and Parmenter, Trevor. "Conceptual Framework for Policy and Research Development With Indigenous People With Disabilities." *Australian Aboriginal Studies*, 2, (2013), 42–58.

Gitlin, Todd. *The Whole World is Watching: Mass Media in the Making and Unmaking of the New Left*. Berkeley: University of California Press. (1980).

Gonzales, Angela. "The (Re)Articulation of American Indian Identity: Maintaining Boundaries and Regulating Access to Ethnically Tied Resources." *American Indian Culture & Research Journal*, 22(4) (December 1998), 199–225.

Gorin, Nicholas S. "Casting a New Light on Tribal Casino Gaming: Why Congress Should Curtail the Scope of High Stakes Indian Gaming." *Cornell Law Review*, 84(3) (1999), 798–849.

Graham, James. "He Apiti Hono, He Tatai Hono: That Which is Joined Remains an Unbroken Line: Using Whakapapa (Genealogy) as the Basis for an Indigenous Research Framework." *Australian Journal of Indigenous Education*, 34: (July 22, 2015), 86–95.

Gray, Jim. "Standing Rock: The Biggest Story That No One's Covering." *Indian Country Today*. (September 13, 2018). Retrieved at http://indian-countrymedianetwork.com/

Green, Barbara. "VA. Indians Past Present Future 'We are One People Says Chief, Physician." *Richmond Times Dispatch*. (August 24, 1987).

Green, Donna, Jack Billy and Alo Tapim. "Indigenous Australians' Knowledge of Weather and Climate." *Climatic Change*, 100(2) (2010), 337–354. https://doi.org/10.1007/s10584-010-9803-z.

Grua, David. *Surviving Wounded Knee: The Lakotas and the Politics of Memory*. New York, NY: Oxford University Press. (2016).

Hackett, Robert A., Susan Forde, Shane Gunster and Kerrie Foxwell-Norton. *Journalism and Climate Crisis: Public Engagement, Media Alternatives*. New York: Routledge. (2017).

Hall, Stuart. "Culture, Media and the "Ideological Effect." In Curran, J., Michael Gurevich, and Janet Wollacott (Eds.), *Mass Communication and Society*. London: Edward Arnold. (1977).

Hall, Stuart. "The Whites of Their Eyes: Racist Ideologies and the Media." In Dines, Gail and Jean M. Humez (Eds.), *Gender, Race and Class in Media*, vol. 1. Thousand Oaks, CA: Sage. (1995). 18.

Hallahan, Kirk. "Seven Models of Framing: Implications for Public Relations." *Journal of Public Relations Research*, 11(3) (1999), 205–242.

Hallin, Daniel C. *The "Uncensored" War: The Media and Vietnam*. New York: Oxford University Press. (1986).

Hallin, Daniel. "Hegemony: The American News Media from Vietnam to El Salvador, a Study of Ideological Change and Its Limits." In David Paletz (Ed.), *Political Communication Research*. Norwood, NJ: Ablex. (1987). 3–25.

Hanson, Jeffry R. and Linda P. Rouse, L. P. "Dimensions of Native American Stereotyping." *American Indian Culture and Research Journal*, 11(4), (1987), 33–58.

Harding, Sandra. "Comment on Hekman's 'Truth and Method: Feminist Standpoint Theory Revisited': Whose Standpoint Needs the Regimes of Truth and Reality?" *22 Signs* (Winter 1997), 382.

Harris, Mavis. "2019 Indian Gross Gaming Revenues of $34.6B Set Industry Record and Show a 2.5% Increase." National Indian Gaming Commission, Gaming Revenue Reports. (Dec. 8, 2020) https://www.nigc.gov/news/detail/2019-indian-gross-gaming-revenues-of-34.6b-set-industry-record-and-show-a-2.5-increase.

Hartman, Leda., Linda Wertheimer, and Noah Adams. "Nativeness." *NPR All Things Considered*. (July 20, 1998).

Hartsock, Nancy C.M. "Comment on Hekman's 'Truth and Method: Feminist Standpoint Theory Revisited': Truth or Justice?" *22 Signs* (Winter 1997), 367.

Harvard Project on American Indian Economic Development. "Harvard Project on American Indian Economic Development Releases Research on Allocation of COVID-19 Response Funds." (April 13, 2020). https://ash.harvard.edu/news/harvard-project-american-indian-economic-development-releases-research-and-ecommendations?utm_medium=Email&utm_campaign=HPAIED+COVID+Recommendations&utm_source=Press.

Heider, Don. *White News: Why Local News Programs Don't Cover People of Color*. London: Routledge. (2000).

Heim, Joe. "How a Long-Dead White Supremacist Still Threatens the Future of Virginia's Indian Tribes." *The Washington Post*. (June 30, 2015).

Heim, Joe. "An Identity Denied." *The Washington Post*. (July 2, 2015).

Hill, Latoya and Samantha Artiga. "COVID-19 Vaccination Among American Indian and Alaska Native People." *Kaiser Family Foundation* (April, 9, 2021). https://www.kff.org/racial-equity-and-health-policy/issue-brief/covid-19-vaccination-american-indian-alaska-native-people/.

"House Vote Recognizes Sovereignty of Virginia Tribe." *The Circle: News from an American Indian Perspective*. (June 6, 2007).

"How Jim Crow Practiced Paper Genocide Against Native American Indians" (2016). Retrieved from https://www.dailykos.com/stories/2016/6/25/1542478/-How-Jim-Crow-Practiced- Paper-Genocide-Against-Native-American-Indians.
Hsu, Spencer S. "Possibility of Casinos Splits Va.; Indian Autonomy Plan Faces Fight in Congress." *The Washington Post*. (September 16, 2000). A1.
Hunt, Darek. "BIA's Impact on Indian Education is an Education in Bad Education." *Indian Country Today*. (Jan. 30, 2012). Retrieved from https://indiancountrymedianetwork.com/news/bias-impact-on-indian-education-is-an-education-in-bad-education/.
Indian Country Defined 18 U.S. Code § 1151.
"Indians Plan to Protest at Jamestown Anniversary if Not Recognized as Tribe." *Wind River News*. (Dec 22, 2005).
Indian Self-Determination and Education Assistance 25 U.S.C. § 450.
Iyengar, Shanto. *Is Anyone Responsible? How Television Frames Political Issues*. Chicago: University of Chicago Press. (1991).
Iyengar, Shanto and Donald Kinder. *News That Matters: Television and American Opinion*. Chicago, IL: University of Chicago Press. (1987).
Iyengar, Shanto and Kyu Hahn. "Red Media, Blue Media: Evidence of Ideological Selectivity in Media Use." *Journal of Communication* 59(1) (March 2009), 19–39.
Jaimes, M. Annette. "Federal Indian Identification Policy: A Usurpation of Indigenous Sovereignty in North America." In M. Annette Jaimes (Ed.), *The State of Native America: Genocide, Colonization and Resistance*. Boston, MA: South End Press. (1992). 123–138.
Jamieson, Kathleen Hall and Joseph N. Cappella. "The Role of the Press in the Health Care Reform Debate of 1993–1994." In Graber, Doris, Dennis McQuail, & Pippa Norris (Eds.), *The Politics of News: The News of Politics*. Washington, DC: CQ Press. (1998). 129–130.
Jobe, Margaret M. "Native Americans and the U.S. Census: A Brief Historical Survey." *Journal of Government Information*, 30 (2004), 66–80.
Johnson, Sally. "Abenakis' Chief Pursues Cause Through Conflict." *New York Times* (October 2, 1988). Sect. 1, 46.
Kahakalau, Ku. "Indigenous Heuristic Action Research: Bridging Western and Indigenous Research Methodologies." *Hulili: Multidisciplinary Research on Hawaiian Well-Being*, 1(1) (2004), 91–103.
Kappler, Charles Joseph and the United States. Indian Affairs, Laws and Treaties (United States. Congress. Senate) ([2d ed.].). G.P.O. (1904).
Kellner, Douglas. *Television and the Crisis of Democracy*. Boulder, CO: Westview. (1990).
Kelly Casey R. "Orwellian Language and the Politics of Tribal Termination (1953–1960)." *Western Journal of Communication*, 74(4) (July 19, 2010), 351–371.
Kinsella, Jim. Interviewed by Azocar, Cristina on March 12, 2021.
Klopotek, Brian. *Recognition Odysseys: Indigeneity, Race, and Federal Tribal Recognition Policy in Three Louisiana Indian Communities*. Durham, NC: Duke University Press. (2011).

Kovach, Margaret. *Indigenous Methodologies: Characteristics, Conversations and Contexts*. University of Toronto Press. (2009).
Kroft, Steve. "Wampum Wonderland." CBS News, *60 Minutes*. (September 18, 1994).
Krol, Deb. Interviewed by Azocar, Cristina on February 9, 2021.
Lach, Donald F. *Asia in the Making of Europe, Volume 1: The Century of Discovery*. Chicago, IL: University of Chicago Press. (1965).
Lacroix, Celeste C. "High Stakes Stereotypes: The Emergence of the 'Casino Indian' Trope in Television's Depictions of Contemporary Native Americans." *The Howard Journal of Communications*, 22(1) (2011), 1–23. https://doi.org/10.1080/10646175.2011.546738
LaPoe, Victoria and Benjamin LaPoe, B. *Indian Country: Telling a Story in a Digital Age*. Michigan State Press: Lansing, MI. (2017).
LaPoe, Victoria, Candi S. Carter, and Benjamin LaPoe, B. *Underserved Communities and Digital Discourse*. Lexington Books: New York. (2018).
Larson, Stephanie Greco. *Media & Minorities: The Politics of Race in News and Entertainment*. Lanham, MD: Rowman & Littlefield. (2006).
Latane, Lawrence III. "Tribes Go Against U.S. Trend Moral, Ethical Values, Red Tape are Concerns." *Richmond Times Dispatch*. (December 11, 1994.)
Leavy, Patricia and Kathryn P. Maloney, K. "Newspaper Coverage of the Columbine and Red Lake School Shootings: Collective Memory, School Violence and 'People Like Us.'" *Critical Sociology*, 35(2) (2009), 273–292.
Lewerenz, Dan. Interviewed by Azocar, Cristina on March 22, 2021.
Linsky, Martin. *Impact: How the Press Affects Federal Policy Making*. New York, NY: W. W. Norton. (1986).
Littlefield, D. F., and Parins, J. W. *American Indian and Alaska Native Newspapers and Periodicals, 1925–1970*. New York, NY: Greenwood. (1984).
Locklear, Arlinda interviewed by Azocar, Cristina on March 23, 2021.
Loew, Patty. "Finding a New Voice—Foundations for American Indian Media." In Carstarphen, Meta and John Sanchez (Eds.), *American Indians and the Mass Media*. Norman, OK: University of Oklahoma Press. (2011). 3–6.
Loew, Patty and Kelly Mella, "Black Ink and the New Red Power: Native American Newspapers and Tribal Sovereignty." *Journalism & Communication Monographs*, 7(3) (Sept. 1, 2005), 99–142. https://doi.org/info:doi/
Louishomme, Claude. 2003. "Competing for Growth: The Exceptional Case of Gaming: PROD." *The American Behavioral Scientist*, 46(8) (04), 1104–1125.
Luna-Firebaugh, Eileen M. and Mary Jo Tippeconnic Fox. 2010. "The Sharing Tradition Indian Gaming in Stories and Modern Life." *Wicazo Sa Review*, 25(1), 75–86.
Lyden, Jacki and John Ydstie. "Effort of the Schaghticoke Tribal Nation as They Seek Federal Recognition from the Bureau of Indian Affairs." NPR, *All Things Considered*. (October 29, 2002).
Marshall, Joshuah. "Tribal Nations—Highly Vulnerable to COVID-19—Need More Federal Relief, Off the Charts Center on Budget and Policy Priorities." Center on Budget and Policy Priorities. (April 1, 2020).

Martin, Karen L. *Please Knock Before You Enter: Aboriginal Regulation of Outsiders and the Implications for Research*. Teneriffe QLD: Post Pressed. (2008).
Martini, Michelle. "Online Distant Witnessing and Live-Streaming Activism: Emerging Differences in the Activation of Networked Publics." *New Media & Society*, 20(11) (2018), 4035–4055.
Maryland-Virginia Compact Act of 1785. "Slaves, Free Negroes and Mulattoes." Virginia Acts § 5.11 (1785).
Mashpee Wampanoag Tribe. https://mashpeewampanoagtribe-nsn.gov/. Accessed March 16, 2021.
Mason, Clark. "Tribe Expansion Scrutinized in Windsor." *The Press Democrat*, Santa Rosa, CA (June 20, 2011).
Matte, Jacqueline Anderson. "Extinction by Reclassification: The MOWA Choctaws of South Alabama and Their Struggle for Federal Recognition." *The Alabama Review*, 59(3), (2006), 163–204.
Matthiessen, Hines. *Wildlife in America*. New York: Viking Press. (1959).
McCombs, Maxwell E. and Donald L. Shaw. "The Agenda-Setting Function of Mass Media." *Public Opinion Quarterly*, 36(2), (1972), 176–187. Retrieved from https://doi.org/10.1086/267990.
McCombs, Maxwell E. and George Estrada. "The News Media and the Pictures in Our Heads." In Iyengar, Shanto and Richard, Reeves (Eds.), *Do the Media Govern? Politicians, Voters and Reporters in America*. Thousand Oaks, CA: Sage. (1997). 237–247.
McCombs, Maxwell and Salma I. Ghanem. "The Convergence of Agenda Setting and Framing." In Reese, Stephen, D., Oscar H. Gandy, and August. E. Grant (Eds.), *Framing Public Life: Perspectives on Media and Our Understanding of the Social World*. Mahwah, NJ: Lawrence Erlbaum. (2001). 67–82.
McCulloch, Anne Merlene and David E. Wilkins, D. E. "'Constructing' Nations Within States: The Quest for Federal Recognition by the Catawba and Lumbee Tribes." *American Indian Quarterly*, 19(3) (Summer, 1995), 361–388.
Mesce, Deborah. *A PRB Media Landscape Review: Are the News Media Giving Policymakers the Information They Need?* Washington, DC: Population Reference Bureau. (March 20, 2018).
Miller, Autumn and Susan Dente Ross. "They Are Not Us: Framing of American Indians by the Boston Globe." *Howard Journal of Communication*, 15(4) (August 11, 2010), 245–259.
Miller, Joanne M. "Examining the Mediators of Agenda Setting: A New Experimental Paradigm Reveals the Role of Emotions." *Political Psychology*, 28(6) (2007), 689–717.
Miller, Mitchell E. "400 Years is Long Enough: Virginia's First Contact Indian Tribes Demand Federal Recognition." *Sunday Gazette—Mail*. (May 28, 2017).
Mills, Kateleigh. "All Oklahoma Tribal Casinos Closed to Mitigate COVID-19." *KOSU*, Stillwater, OK. (March 23, 2020).
Mitchell, Amy. Jeffrey Gottfried, Jocelyn Kiley, and Katerina Eva Matsa. "Section 1: Media Resources: Distinct Favorites Emerge on the Left and Right." *Pew Research Center: Journalism & Media* (October 21, 2014). Retrieved from http://www

.journalism.org/2014/10/21/section-1-media-sources-distinct-favorites-emerge-on-the-left-and-right/.

Monet, Jenni. "The Crisis in Covering Indian Country." *Columbia Journalism Review* (March 29, 2019). Retrieved from https://www.cjr.org/opinion/Indigenous-journalism-erasure.php.

Moore, Ellen. *Journalism, Politics, and the Dakota Access Pipeline: Standing Rock and the Framing of Injustice.* New York, NY: Routledge. (2018).

Moore, Ellen E. and Kylie R. Lanthorn. "Framing Disaster: News Media Coverage of Two Native American Environmental Justice Cases." *Journal of Communication Inquiry*, 41(3) (July 2017), 227–249. https://doi.org/10.1177/0196859917706348.

Morison, Samuel Eliot. *The European Discovery of America: The Southern Voyages, A.D. 1492–1616.* New York, NY: Oxford University Press. (1974).

Murphy Sharon M. "Journalism in Indian Country: Story Telling That Makes Sense." *Howard Journal of Communications*, 21(4) (November 19, 2010), 328–344.

Murray, Paul T. "Who Is an Indian? Who Is a Negro? Virginia Indians in the World War II Draft." *The Virginia Magazine of History and Biography*, 95(2) (1987), 215–231.

Nagle, Rebecca. "This Land." *Crooked Media Podcast 2021.* Retrieved from https://crooked.com/podcast-series/this-land/.

Nakata, Martin. "Anthropological Texts and Indigenous Standpoints." *Australian Aboriginal Studies,* 2 (1998), 3.

Nakata, Martin. "Indigenous Knowledge and the Cultural Interface: Underlying Issues at the Intersection of Knowledge and Information Systems." In Hickling-Hudson, Anne, Julie Matthews and Annette. Wood (Eds). *Disrupting Preconceptions: Postcolonialism and Education.* Flaxton, Queensland: Post Pressed. (2004). 19–38.

Nakata, Martin (2007) 'The cultural interface' 36 (Supplement) Australian Journal of Indigenous Education 7.

National Conference of State Legislators. (2020). https://www.ncsl.org/research/state-tribal-institute/list-of-federal-and-state-recognized-tribe.aspx#State. Accessed May 7, 2020.

National Congress of American Indians. (2020). "Gaming." https://www.ncai.org/policy-issues/economic-development-commerce/gaming.

National Indian Gaming Commission. "Gaming Revenue Reports." Retrieved from www.nigc.gov/TribalDate/tabid/67/Default.aspx.

Native American Journalists Association. "History." https://najanewsroom.com/mission-and-history/. Accessed March 8, 2021.

Native American Journalists Association. "Reporting Guides." https://najanewsroom.com/reporting-guides/.

Native American Rights Fund. https://www.narf.org/. Accessed March 2, 2021.

Naylor, Brian. "U.S. Grants Federal Recognition to Pamunkey Indian Tribe." NPR, *All Things Considered.* (July 2, 2015).

Newland, Bryan. U.S. Congress Senate Committee on Indian Affairs. Testimony of Senior Policy Advisor Office of the Assistant Secretary For Indian Affairs, United States Department of the Interior to the Committee on Indian Affairs United States

Senate. Oversight Hearing on Federal Acknowledgement: Political and Legal Relationship Between Governments. (July 12, 2012).

New Mexico State Government. "Tribal Casinos Close Due to COVID-19." NewMexico.gov. (March 19, 2020). https://www.newmexico.gov/2020/03/19/tribal-casinos-close-due-to-covid-19/.

Norris, Tina, Paula L. Vines and Elizabeth M. Hoeffel, E. M. "The American Indian and Alaska Native Population: 2010." *U.S. Census Bureau*. C2010-BR10. (2012). Office of the Assistant Secretary of Indian Affairs. Press Release.

O'Heffernan, Patrick. *Mass Media and American Foreign Policy: Insider Perspective on Global Journalism and Foreign Policy Process*. Norwood, NJ: Ablex. (1991).

Osburn, Katherine M.B. "The 'Identified Full-Bloods' in Mississippi: Race and Choctaw Identity, 1898–1918." *Ethnohistory*, 56(3) (2009), 423–447.

Our Documents. "Dawes Act 1887." OurDocuments.gov. (N.D.) Retrieved from https://www.ourdocuments.gov/doc.php?flash=true&doc=50.

"Overdue Recognition: Six American Indian Tribe in Virginia Deserve to Be Acknowledged by the U.S." (editorial). *Norfolk Daily Press*. (September 22, 2016).

Paletz, David. "The Media and Public Policy." In Graber, Doris, Dennis McQuail and P. Norris (Eds.), *The Politics of News: The News of Politics*. Washington DC: CQ. (1998). 218–237.

Pan, Zhougdang and Gerald Kosicki. "Framing Analysis: An Approach to News discourse." *Political Communication*, 10 (1993), 55–75.

Patterson, Thomas E. 2016. "News Coverage of the 2016 Presidential Primaries: Horse Race Reporting Has Consequences." Shorenstein Center, July 11. https://shorensteincenter.org/news-coverage-2016-presidential-primaries/.

Peters, Paula. Interviewed by Azocar, Cristina on March 8, 2021.

Peterson, Iver. "Would-be Tribes Entice Investors," *New York Times*. (March 29, 2004). Retrieved from https://www.nytimes.com/2004/03/29/nyregion/would-be-tribe-entice-investors.html. Accessed March 23, 2021.

Pevar, Stephen L. *The Rights of Indians and Tribes: The Authoritative ACLU Guide to Indian and Tribal Rights* (3rd ed.). Carbondale, IL: Southern Illinois University Press. (2002).

Pevar, Stephen L. *The Rights of Indians and Tribes*. New York, NY: New York University Press. (2004).

Philp, Kenneth R. *John Collier's Crusade for Indian Reform, 1920–1954*. Tucson, AZ: University of Arizona Press. (1977).

Pilger, John. *Hidden Agendas*. London: Vintage. (1988), 3.

Pindus, Nancy M., G. Thomas Kingsley, Jennifer Biess, Diane K. Levy, Jasmine Simington and Christopher R. Hayes. "Housing Needs of American Indians and Alaska Natives in Tribal Areas." *Urban Institute*. (January 19, 2017). Retrieved from https://www.urban.org/research/publication/housing-needs-american-indians-and-alaska-natives-tribal-areas.

Pollard, Bryan. Interviewed by Azocar, Cristina on February 3, 2021.

Pollard, Bryan. "More Than News, Indigenous Media Empowers Native Voices and Communities." *American Indian*, 21(2) (2020). https://www.americanindianmagazine.org/story/Indigenous-media.

Porsanger, Jelena 2004. "An Essay About Indigenous Methodology." Nordlit; Working Papers in Literature 2004: Special Issue on Northern Minorities. (2004), 105–120. Accessed August 13. http://uit.no/getfile.php?PageId=977%FileId=188.

Price, Vincent and David Tewksbury. "News Values and Public Opinion: A Theoretical Account of Media Priming and Framing." In Barnett, George and Franklin J. Boster (Eds.), *Progress in the Communication Sciences*. Greenwich, CT: Ablex. (1997). 173–212.

Preston, David. "Table of Contents." In *The Texture of Contact: European and Indian Settler Communities on the Frontiers of Iroquoia, 1167–1783 (The Iroquoians and Their World)*. London: University of Nebraska Press. (2009). V–Vi. doi:10.2307/j.ctt1dgn465.2

Publick Occurrences Both Forreign and Domestick. (September 25, 1690). Retrieved from http://nationalhumanitiescenter.org/pds/amerbegin/power/text5/PublickOccurrences.pdf.

Quinn, William W. "Federal Acknowledgment of American Indian Tribes The Historical Development of a Legal Concept." *The American Journal of Legal History*, 34(4) (1990), 331–364. https://doi.org/10.2307/845826.

Reese, Stephen D. "Prologue—Framing Public Life: A Bridging Model for Media Research." In Reese, Stephen D., Oscar H. Gandy, and August E. Grant (Eds.), *Framing Public Life: Perspectives on Media and Our Understanding of the Social World*. Mahwah, NJ, Lawrence Erlbaum. (2001). 7–32.

Rigney, Lester-Irabinna. "A First Perspective of Indigenous Australian Participation in Science: Framing Indigenous Research towards Indigenous Intellectual Sovereignty." *Second National Indigenous Researchers Forum*, Adelaide, University of South Australia. (1997).

Rigney, Lester-Irabinna. "Internalisation of an Indigenous Anti-Colonial Cultural Critique of Research Methodologies. A Guide to Indigenous Research Methodologies and its Principles." *Journal of American Studies*, 14(2), (1997). 109–122.

Rigney, Lester-Irabinna. "The First Perspective: Culturally Safe Research Practices On or With Indigenous Peoples." In *1999 Chacmool Conference Proceedings*. University of Calgary, Alberta, Canada. (1999).

Rister, C.C. "The Significance of the Destruction of the Buffalo in the Southwest." *Southwestern Historical Quarterly*, 33(1) (1929), 34–49.

Robertson, D. F. "Time to Abolish the Bureau? Proposed Legislative Response to BIA Abuses at CNO." *Cherokee Observer*. (2012). Retrieved from http://www.cherokeeobserver.org/Issues/abolishbiapart1.html.

Robertson, Dwana L. "The Myth of Indian Casino Riches." *Indian Country Today* (April 19, 2017). Retrieved from https://newsmaven.io/indiancountrytoday/archive/the-myth-of-indian- casino-riches-3H8eP-wHX0Wz0H4WnQjwjA/.

Rokeach, Milton. *The Open & Closed Mind: Investigations Into the Nature of Belief Systems and Personality Systems*. New York, NY: Basic Books. (1960).

Romano, Jay. "3 Indian Tribes Stir Casino Fears." *New York Times*. (August 1, 1993).

Rossum, Ralph A. *The Supreme Court and Tribal Gaming:* California v. Cabazon Band of Mission Indians. Lawrence, KA: University Press of Kansas. (2011).

Rountree, Helen C. "The Indians of Virginia: A Third Race in a Biracial State." In Williams, Walter L. (Ed.), *Southeastern Indians Since the Removal Era*. Athens: University of Georgia Press. (1979) pp. 27–48.

Rountree, Helen C. *Pocahontas's People: The Powhatan Indians of Virginia Through Four Centuries*. Norman, OK: University of Oklahoma Press. (1990).

Rountree, Helen C. *The Powhatan Indians of Virginia: Their Traditional Culture*. Norman, OK: University of Oklahoma Press. (1992).

Rountree, Helen C. and E. Randolph Turner III. *Before and After Jamestown: Virginia's Powhatans and Their Predecessors*. Gainesville, FL: University Press of Florida. (2002).

Rural Health Information Hub. "Rural Tribal Health." Retrieved from https://www.ruralhealthinfo.org/topics/rural-tribal-health. Accessed April 4, 2019.

Russel, Annelise, Maraam Dwidar, and Bryan D. Jones. "The Mass Media and the Policy Process." *Oxford Research Encyclopedia of Politics* (August 31, 2016). doi: 10.1093/acrefore/9780190228637.013.240

Saunders, Debra J. "The Jackpot Casino Carmel Tribe?" *The San Francisco Chronicle* (February 14, 2001) A25.

Schilling, Vincent. "Six VA Tribes Slotted for Federal Recognition as Senators Warner & Kaine Secure Bill Passage." *Indian Country Today*. (September 13, 2018) Retrieved from Six VA Tribes Slotted For Federal Recognition as Senators Warner & Kaine Secure Bill Passage—Indian Country Today.

Schmidt, Ryan W. "American Indian Identity and Blood Quantum in the 21st Century: A Critical Review." *Journal of Anthropology*, 5 (2011), 5. Retrieved from http://dx.doi.org/10.1155/2011/549521.

Schudson, Michael. *The Sociology of News* (2nd ed.). New York, NY: W. W. Norton & Company. (2011).

Shah, Dhavan V., Douglas M. McLeod, Melissa R. Gotlieb, and Nam-Jin Lee. "Framing and Agenda Setting." In Nabi, Robin L. and Mary Beth Oliver (Eds.), *The SAGE Handbook of Media Processes and Effects*. Thousand Oaks, CA: Sage. (2009). 83–98.

Shaughnessy, Tim. "White Stereotypes of Indians." *Journal of American Indian Education*, 17(2) (1978), 20–24.

Shear, Sara B., Ryan T. Knowles, Gregory Soden, and Antonio Castro. "Manifesting Destiny: Representations of Indigenous Peoples in K-12 U.S. History Standards." *Research in Social Education*, 43(1) (February 19, 2015), 68–101.

Shefveland, Kristalynn Marie. *Anglo-Native Virginia: Trade, Conversion, and Indian Slavery in The Old Dominion, 1646-1722*. Athens: University of Georgia Press. (2016).

Smith, Anna V. "Casino closures in Indian Country Hit Core Tribal Services." *High Country News*. (April 10, 2020). Retrieved from https://www.hcn.org/articles/covid19-casino-closures-in-indian-country-hit-core-tribal-services.

Smith, Dorothy E. "Comment on Hekman's 'Truth and Method: Feminist Standpoint Theory Revisited.'" *Signs*, 22 (1997), 392.

Smith, J. David. *The Eugenic Assault on America: Scenes in Red, White, and Black*. Fairfax, VA: George Mason University Press. (1992).

Smith, Jake, John McCarthy, Clark McPhail, and Boguslaw Augustyn, "From Protest to Agenda Building: Description Bias in Media Coverage of Protest Events in Washington, D.C." *Social Forces*, 79(4) (2001), 1397–1423.

Smith, Tuhiwai L. "Kaupapa Maori Methodology: Our Power to Define Ourselves." (1999). Accessed January 25, 2020. http://www.hauora.com/RESEARCH/PUBLISHED/KaupapaMaoriMethodology/tabi.

Smith, Tuhiwai L. Decolonizing Methodologies, Red Talks, San Francisco State University. (February 11, 2021). https://www.youtube.com/watch?v=bboxzss_PxM&feature=youtu.be. Accessed February 23, 2021.

Smith, Tuhiwai L. *Decolonizing Methodologies: Research and Indigenous People*. London: Zed Books. (1999).

Spitzer, Robert (Ed.). *Media and Public Policy*. Westport, CT: Praeger. (1993).

Spruhan, Paul. "A Legal History of Blood Quantum in Federal Indian Law to 1935." *South Dakota Law Review*, 51(1) (2006), 1–50.

Srinivasan, Ancha. "Local and Indigenous Knowledge (LINK) for Adaptation to Climate Change." Institute for Global Environment Strategies, Japan (October, 2004).

Staff Reports. "History of the Cherokee Phoenix." *CherokeePhoenix.org*. (2015). Accessed March 5, 2021. https://www.cherokeephoenix.org/archives/history-of-the-cherokee-phoenix/article_30c25bf9-bc26-5628-9687-75e1be8581ba.html.

Stannard, David E. *American Holocaust: The Conquest of the New World*. New York, NY: Oxford University Press. (1993).

Steihnauer, Evelyn. "Thoughts on an Indigenous Research Methodology." *Canadian Journal of Education*, 26(2): (2002), 69–81.

Stensland, Anna Lee. "Indian Writers and Indian Lives." *Equity & Excellence in Education*, 12(6), (1974), 3–7.

Stossel, John. "A Nation of Freeloaders?" Fox Business Network. (July 5, 2012).

Sunuwar, Dev Kumar. "Indigenous Media Caucus Amplifies Indigenous Voices Globally." *Cultural Survival*. (September 19, 2019). Retrieved from https://www.culturalsurvival.org/news/Indigenous-media-caucus-amplifies-Indigenous-voices-globally.

Talahongva, Patty. Interviewed by Azocar, Cristina on February 23, 2021.

TallBear, Kim. "DNA, Blood and Racializing the Tribes." In Ifekwunigwe, J. (Ed.), *Mixed Race Studies: A Reader*. New York, NY: Routledge. (2004). 123.

Tallent, Rebecca. "Don't Misrepresent Native Americans." *The Quill*, 101 (2013), 26.

Tate, Joseph. *Digest of the Laws of Virginia Which Are of a Permanent Character and General Operation* (2nd ed.). Richmond, VA: Smith and Palmer (1841). Retrieved from https://books.google.com/books?id=TqZXAAAAcAAJ&pg=PA843&lpg=PA843&dq=%5BE%5Dvery+person+of+whose+grandfathers+or+grandmothers+any+one+is+or+shall+have+been+a+Negro,+although+all+his+other+progenitors,+except+that+descending+from+the+Negro+shall+have+been+white+persons+.+.+.+and+so+every+person+who+shall+have+one-fourth+or+more&source=bl&ots=p6--zQ4HHj&sig=ACfU3U2RHTx7HzXSc5Svvfxm5gkhCmGW2A&hl=en&sa=X&ved=2ahUKEwjHvfa346LhAhUoIDQIHe9ABD0Q6AEwAXoECAkQAQ#v=onepage&q&f=true.

Tejon Indian Tribe website. "Our History." Accessed February 15, 2021. https://www.tejonindiatribe.com/our-history/.
Timbisha Shoshone Tribe website. Accessed February 15, 2021. http://www.timbisha.org/.
Tipa, Gail, Ruth Panelli, and the Moeraki Stream Team. "Beyond 'Some Else's Agenda': An Example of Indigenous/Academic Research Collaboration." *New Zealand Geographer* 65(95) (July 23, 2009), 95–106. doi:10.1111/j.1745-7939.2009.01152.x.
Toensing, Gail Courtney. "Mashpee Wampanoag in New Kien Huat Partnership." *Indian Country Today* (December 9, 2009). Retrieved from https://indiancountrytoday.com/archive/mashpee-wampanoag-in-new-kien-huat-partnership.
Tompkins, Hilary Tribal Treaty and Environmental Statutory Implications of the Dakota Access Pipeline. (December 4, 2016). Office of the Solicitor Memorandum.
Trahant, Mark. "A Tribe With a View." In Rolo, Mark Anthony (Ed.), *The American Indian and the Media* (2nd ed.). New York, NY: The National Conference for Community and Justice. (2000). 32–35.
U.S. Census Office. *The Seventh Census of the United States: 1850*. Washington, D.C.: R. Armstrong, Public Printer. (1853).
U.S. Congress. House. Encouraging Indian Economic Development to Provide for the Disclosure of Indian Tribal Sovereign Immunity in Contracts Involving Indian Tribes, and for Other Purposes. Report from the Committee on Indian Affairs. Rep. No. 1804, at 6 (1934).
U.S. Congress. House. To Provide the Timbisha Shoshone Tribe a Permanent Land Base Within Its Aboriginal Homeland, and Other Purposes. H.R. 5322—106th Congress. Introduced February 24, 2000. www.GovTrack.us. 2000. https://www.govtrack.us/congress/bills/106/hr5322.
U.S. Congress. Senate. Committee on Indian Affairs. Thomasina Jordan Indian Tribes of Virginia Federal Recognition Act and the Grand River Band of Ottawa Indians of Michigan Referral Act Hearing before the Committee on Indian Affairs United States 109th congress, Second Session, S. 437 and S. 480, June 21, 2006. Washington, D.C. Available at https://www.gpo.gov/fdsys/pkg/CHRG-109shrg28348/html/CHRG-109shrg28348.htm.
U.S. Department of Health and Human Services. Office of Minority Health. "Profile: American Indian/Alaska Native." (May 21, 2021). https://www.minorityhealth.hhs.gov/omh/browse.aspx?lvl=3&lvlid=62.
U.S. Department of the Interior. Bureau of Indian Affairs. 2020 CARES Act: Bureau of Indian Education Virtual Listening Session—July 8. Washington, D.C. (2020). https://www.bia.gov/covid-19/cares-act.
U.S. Department of the Interior. Bureau of Indian Affairs. "Acquisition of Lands, Water Rights or Surface Rights; Appropriation; Title to Lands; Tax Exemption." (January 1, 2018). Section 465 25 U.S.C. §§ 463, 465.
U.S. Department of the Interior, Bureau of Indian Affairs. "CA Rancheria Terminated By the BIA" Press Release. (November 12, 1965) https://www.bia.gov/as-ia/opa/online-press-release/ca-rancheria-terminated-bia#.

U.S. Department of the Interior. Bureau of Indian Affairs. "Tribal Nations Benefits and Service." Retrieved from https://www.doi.gov/tribes/benefits.

U.S. Department of the Interior. Bureau of Indian Affairs. Procedures for Establishing that an American Group Exists as a Tribe. Code of Federal Regulations 25 CFR § 83. (2017).

U.S. Department of the Interior. Department of Indian Affairs. Procedures for Establishing that an American Indian Group Exists as an Indian Tribe: Mandatory Requirement for Federal Acknowledgement. Code of Federal Regulations 25 CFR § 83.7.

U.S. Department of the Interior. Department of the Interior Announces Final Federal Recognition Process to Acknowledge Indian Tribes. Press release. (June 6/29/2015). Retrieved from https://www.doi.gov/pressreleases/department-interior-announces-final-federal-recognition-process-acknowledge-indian-tribes.

U.S. Government Accountability Office. "Indian Issues: Federal Funding for Non-Federally Recognized Tribes." (April 12, 2012). Retrieved from http://www.gao.gov/products/GAO-12-348.

U.S. Government Accountability Office. "National Environmental Policy Act: Little Information Exists on NEPA Analyses" Press Release. (April, 14, 2014). GAO-14-369.

U.S. Statutes at large Number (1898): 30:495.

Untitled news story about the Native Hawaiian Akaka bill. KFVE-TV, Honolulu, HI. (May 3, 2010).

United States National Advisory Commission on Civil Disorders. *The Kerner Report: The 1968 Report of the National Advisory Commission on Civil Disorders.* New York, NY: Pantheon Books. (1988).

Walker, Judith and Pierre Walter, P. "Learning About Social Movements Through News Media: Deconstructing *New York Times* and Fox News Representations of Standing Rock." *International Journal of Lifelong Education*, 37(4) (2018), 401–418.

Wanamaker, Tom. "Let the Games Begin: Anti-Gamers Rail Against Recognition; A Threat to Tribal Economics." *Indian Country Today*. (September 4, 2002).

Waugaman, Sandra F. and Danielle Moretti-Langholtz, D. *We're Still Here: Contemporary Virginia Indians Tell Their Stories.* Richmond, VA: Palari Publishing. (2000).

Weber-Pillwax, Cora. "What is Indigenous Research?" *Canadian Journal of Native Education,* 25(2) (2001), 166–174.

Westin, Mary Ann. *Native Americans In the News: Images of Indians in the Twentieth Century Press.* Westport, CT: Greenwood Press. (1996).

Whelan, Robbie. "Native-American Tribes Pull Ahead in Covid-19 Vaccinations." *Wall Street Journal.* (April 10, 2021). https://www.wsj.com/articles/native-american-tribes-pull-ahead-in-covid-19-vaccinations-11618047001.

Whitford, Emma. "Judge Sends Chinook Suit Against DOI Back To Department." *Law360* (January 22, 2021). Accessed October 24, 2021.

Wilkins, David E. *American Indian Politics and the American Political System.* Lanham, MD: Rowman & Littlefield. (2005).

Wilkins, David E. and Heidi Kiiweitinepinesilk Stark. *American Indian Politics and the American Political System*. Lanham, MD: Rowman & Littlefield. (2011).

Wilkinson, Gerald. "Colonialism Through the Media." *The Indian Historian*, 7(3) (1974), 6.

Wilson, Shawn. "What Is An Indigenous Research Methodology?" *Canadian Journal of Native Education*, 25(2) (2005), 175–179.

Wiltz, Teresa. "Tribes Find Opposition to Gambling the Latest Barrier to Federal Recognition." *News from Indian Country*. (Feb. 8, 2016).

Winokoor, Charles. "Mashpee Wampanoag Still Owes Taunton More Than $530K." *Taunton* (Mass.) *Daily Gazette*. (May 13, 2020). Accessed March 17, 2021. https://www.tauntongazette.com/news/20200513/mashpee-wampanoag-still-owes-taunton-more-than-530k.

Wolfe, Brendan. "Racial Integrity Laws (1924–1930)." In *Encyclopedia Virginia*. (2015). Retrieved from http://www.EncyclopediaVirginia.org/Racial_Integrity_Laws_of_the_1920s.

Wood, Peter H. "The Changing Population of the Colonial South: An Overview by Race and Region, 1685–1790." In Wood, Peter H., Gregory A. Waselkov, and Tom. Hatley (Eds.), *Powhatan's Mantle*. Lincoln, NE: University of Nebraska Press. (1989). 35–103.

Yahr, Natalie. "The Indigenous Affairs News Desk: 'We're the Only Ones in the Room Listening.'" *Center for Journalism Ethics* (January 18, 2021).

"Years of Negotiation End with Land Claim Settlement." *Indian Country Today (1983–1988)*, (November 30, 1983).

Index

1851 Treaty of Fort Laramie, 102

Adkins, Stephen, x
Administrative Procedures Act, 25
agenda setting, 5–6, 8, 37–40, 42, 46–48, 57–58, 61, 63–64, 70, 78, 85
Ahtone, Tristan, 95
Alabama–Coushatta, 108
Alcatraz, 59
Algonquin, 101
Allen, George, 29
American Indian Movement, 38
Anglo-Saxon Clubs of America, 31
anti-miscegenation laws, 71; intermixing, 4, 30–31
Arizona, 38, 102
Arizona House of Representatives, 90
Arizona PBS, 70
The Arizona Republic, xv, 70, 95, 102
Army Corps of Engineers, x, 11
Asian American Journalists Association, xiii, 61
assimilation, 2, 16, 23, 27, 30, 54. *See also* genocide
Au-Authm Action News, 90
authenticity, 13–14, 32–33; braids, 13; feathers, 13; phenotype, 32

BIA. *See* Bureau of Indian Affairs

Bismarck Tribune, 45
blood quantum, 14–17, 22; full-bloods, 17
boarding schools, 16, 38. *See also* genocide
Brown, Kevin, 79
Bureau of Indian Affairs (BIA), 3, 5, 15, 23, 24, 26–27, 29, 64, 71, 78, 80–83, 97–98, 108
Burton, Greg, xv, 102
Bush, George W., 37

Cabazon Band of Mission Indians, 59
California v. Cabazon Band of Mission Indians, 59
Carcieri v. Salazar, 112
The Char-Koosta News, 89, 91
The Cherokee Advocate, 89
The Cherokee Observer, 89
The Cherokee Phoenix, 54, 89, 95, 99
The Cherokee Voice, 90
Chickahominy Tribe, x, 9, 29, 64, 75, 82, 92
Chickasaw, 16
Chinook Indian Nation, 34
Choctaw, 16, 30
The Circle: News from an American Indian Perspective, 89
Class II gaming, 60, 108–109, 111–12

Class III gaming, 60, 110–11
Cleveland, Grover, 16
climate change, 45, 53
Clinton, William J., 98
Coast Miwok, 100
Code of Federal Regulations, 26; 25 CFR Part 83, 25–26; 25 CFR Part 83.11, 27; 25 CFR Part 151, 110; 25 CFR Part 151.1, 110
Cold War, 22
Collier, John, 16, 132
Columbus, Christopher, 13
Committee on Indian Affairs hearing, 60
Communist, 23
Congressional Black Caucus, 79, 81
Cook, Tecumseh Deerfoot, 78
court process, federal acknowledgment by, 26
COVID-19, 24, 53–54, 58–59, 117–18
Cree Deportation Act of 1896, 91
Creek, 16
Curtis Act, 16

Dakota Access Pipeline, 4, 11, 44–45, 58, 60, 101. *See also* Standing Rock; Dakota Access Pipeline
DAPL. *See* Standing Rock; Dakota Access Pipeline
Dawes Act, 2, 14–16; Dawes rolls, 15–16
Dawes, Henry, 15
Democracy Now!, 4
demographics, 32
DOI. *See* U.S. Department of Interior

Eastern Band (of Cherokee Indians), 96
Eastern Chickahominy Tribe, 3, 9, 29, 64, 75, 82
education, 24, 40, 51–53, 59, 71, 97, 99, 117; U.S. education system. *See* genocide
eugenics, 2, 3, 30, 31
Europeans, 13, 41, 75

fake news, 57
Federally Recognized Indian Tribe List Act, 25
Federal Register, 27
Federated Indians of Graton Rancheria, 100
feminist standpoint theory, 52
First Nations Experience (FNX), 70, 88
Fleming, Lee, 27
Florida Bingo Statute, 107
foreclosures, 16
The Fort Apache Scout, 90
Fox News, 45–46, 68, 72, 74
fracking, 45
framing, 5–8, 37–40, 42, 45, 46, 48, 57–58, 61, 63–64, 67, 70, 96; episodic frames, 40, 57; thematic frames, 40
Frazier, Lynn, 16

gaming rights, tribe relinquishing of, 79, 81, 84
Gay Head (Aquinnah) Wampanoag Tribe, 104, 108–109
genocide, 38, 45; assimilation, 2, 16, 23, 27, 30, 54; boarding schools, 16, 38, 118; decimating, 16; enumerators, 32; erasure, 2, 4, 15, 21–22, 28, 30–31, 71; eugenics, 2, 3, 30, 31; intermarried, 17, 32, 71, 80; reclassified, 4, 31; U.S. education system, K-12, 37–38. *See also* paper genocide
Golden Age of diversity, 59
Grand River Band of Ottawa Indians, 62
The Guardian, 46

Halbert v. U.S. 1931, 14
health conditions, 117
Hollywood Seminole Bingo, 107
Hopi, 96
House Bill (HB2889), 32
House Committee on Appropriations, ix, x
House Natural Resources Committee, 84

House Resolution 108, 22
House Resolution 984, 84
hyperdescent, 32

Indian Child Welfare Act, 100
Indian Country Today, v, 44, 70, 88, 90, 92, 95, 100, 103
Indian Gaming Regulatory Act (IGRA), 59–60, 108–109, 111
Indian Reorganization Act (IRA), 14, 17, 21–22, 110–111
Indian Self-Determination and Education Assistance Act of 1975, 1
Indigenous pedagogy, 51
Indigenous standpoint theory (IST), xiv, 6–9, 51–54, 70, 72, 95, 113
Interior Board of Indian Appeals, 28, 80
invisibility, 40, 71
Iowa Tribe of Kansas and Nebraska, xv, 96
Iroquois, 38
IST. *See* Indigenous standpoint theory

Jamestown, x, 75, 92; 2007 celebration of, 79, 84, 92; permanent settlement in America, 61
Jim Crow, 1–3, 17–18, 30
Joint Tribal Council of the Passamaquoddy Tribe v. Morton, 370, 33

Kaine, Tim, 29, 81, 84
Kansas, 38
Kauffman, Hattie, 73
Kerner Report, 59
King William County, 76–77
Kinsella, James, 103
Krol, Deb, xv, 95, 97

legacy media, 57
Lewerenz, Dan, xv, 95–96, 109
liberal journalism, 57
Little Shell Tribe of Chippewa Indians of Montana, 91
Locklear, Arlinda, xv, 1, 23, 28, 109–111, 113

Louisiana, 29, 32
Lumbee, xv, 96

mascots, 58; representations for sports, 59
Mashpee Wampanoag Tribe, 82, 103–104
Massachusetts, 15, 29, 103, 108–109
Matoaka, 3, 76, 82. *See also* Pocahontas
matrilineal, 96, 99
Mattaponi Tribe, 10, 79, 82–83
McCain, John, 60
Métis, 91
MGM Resorts International, 80
Miami Nation of Indians of Indiana, Inc. v. United States Department of Interior, 25
Monacan Indian Nation, 29
Monacan Tribe, 3–4, 9, 64, 75, 82, 92
Myers, Dillon, 23

NAJA. *See* Native American Journalists Association
Nansemond Tribe, 3, 9, 29, 64, 75, 82, 92
NARF. *See* Native American Rights Fund
National Association of Black Journalists, xii, 61
National Defense Authorization Act in 2020, 104
National Harbor Casino Resort, 80
National Indian Gaming Commission (NIGC), 59–60, 108–110
Native American Graves Protection and Repatriation Act, 100
Native American Journalists Association (NAJA), xii, 43, 46, 52, 70, 87, 114–15; NAJA Bingo Card, 46, 114
Native American Times, 89
Native American Press Association, 87. *See also* Native American Journalists Association
Native American Rights Fund (NARF), 96, 99, 104, 109–110
The Native Nevadan, 90

Navajo Times, 89, 92
Nebraska, 38
negative decision, federal recognition, 28, 105, 129
New Echota, 87
New Mexico, 38, 66
News from Indian Country, 89–91
News from Native California, 88–89
News Leaders Association, 70
New York Times, 44–46, 64–66, 71, 114
North Dakota, 45
NPR, 46, 65, 68, 72

OFA. *See* Office of Federal Recognition
Office of Federal Recognition (OFA), 25, 27, 28, 105
Ojibwe Akiing, 90
Ojibwe News, 89
Oklahoma, 38, 118
Oklahoma Indian Times, 89
one drop rule, 31

Pamunkey Tribe, 3, 5, 9, 17–18, 29, 64, 75–85; pursuit of gaming, 85
paper genocide, 4
parachute reporting, 53, 57
Passamaquoddy Tribe, 33
Pequot Times, 89
Peters, Paula, 103, 108, 113
pilgrims, 96, 103
Plecker, Walter Ashby, 3, 31–32, 80, 82. *See also* Virginia Bureau of Vital Statistics
Plymouth Colony, 103
Pocahontas, 3, 76, 82; burial, 400th anniversary of, 81, 84; Warren, Elizabeth, 82
Pollard, Bryan, xv, 51, 95, 97
Potomac River, 78, 80
Powhatan, 75, 77; Chief Powhatan, 76, 82; Powhatan Confederacy, 75, 101, 103
Public Assemblages Act of 1926, 31
public law, 103–454, 25

Racial Integrity Act, 3–4, 30–32, 80
Rappahannock Tribe, 3, 9, 29, 64, 75, 82–84, 92
reaffirmation process, federal acknowledgment by, 29
Reagan, Ronald W., 108
Red Sticks Press, 89
relocation, 23
Removal Era, 30
Report for America, 70
restoration of Tribes, 21, 26, 108
Roosevelt, Franklin D., 16

Sacagawea, 37
Schmit, Cheryl, 80
self-reliance, 23, 58
Seminole Tribe, 16, 107
Seminole Tribe of Florida v. Butterworth, 111
Seminole Tribune, 89, 91–92
Sequoyah, 37, 87
Shakopee Mdewakanton Sioux Tribe, 90
Sho-Ban News, 89–90
Simmons v. Eagle Seelatsee, 14
Sitting Bull, 37, 73
Smith, Linda Tuhiwai, ix, 115
SmokeSygnals. *See* Paula Peters
Southern Pomo, 100
Squanto, 37
Standing Rock, 44; Dakota Access Pipeline, 4, 11, 44, 58, 60, 101; movement, 45; Standing Rock Sioux Tribe, 4; Water Protectors, 44
Stand Up for California, 80
state-recognized tribes, 1, 3, 29, 38, 46, 64
stereotype, 5, 7, 9, 33, 37, 41–42, 46, 53, 70; Affirmative Action, 58; Berkhofer, Robert, 42; braids, 13; casinos, 9, 70, 98; climate change, 53; conservation, 53; criminal, 38, 100; drunk, 38; environmental issues, 53; feathers, 13, 98; language, 73; lazy, 38; moral evaluation, 42;

phrases, 66; vanishing culture, 46; violence, 46

Talahongva, Patty, v, xv, 95–96
tax exemptions, 23
termination, 23, 91
Tester, John, 104
Thanksgiving, 103
Thomasina E. Jordan Indian Tribes of Virginia Federal Recognition Act of 2017, 29
Timbisha Homeland Act, 98
Timbisha Shoshone Tribe, 98
Trahant, Mark, 37, 103
Treaty of Middle Plantation, 102
tribal governments, 16, 21, 59, 71, 96, 99, 115, 118
Tribal Self-Governance Act of 1994, 1
tribal self-reliance, 23, 58
Tribes without federal recognition, 1
tributary tribes, 82, 102
Trump, Donald J., 29, 71, 82, 84
trust responsibility, U.S. government, 24, 34; trust land, 14–15, 97, 103–104, 108–11
Tundra Times, 90

un-people, 40
Upper Mattaponi Indian Tribe, ix, x, 3, 9, 29, 60, 64, 75, 82, 92
urban Indians, 14, 23
U.S. Census, 32; enumerators, 32

U.S. Census Bureau, 2
U.S. Department of the Interior (DOI), 24–25, 29, 77, 105, 109–10
U.S. Marshals, 32
U.S. Secretary of the Interior, 15, 21, 26, 111
U.S. Supreme Court, 1, 4, 59, 97, 107–10

Virginia Bureau of Vital Statistics, 3, 4, 31. *See also* Plecker, Walter Ashby
Virginia Department of Historic Resources, x
Virginia General Assembly, 31, 83, 101

Wahunsenacawh, 76, 82. *See also* Powhatan
Wampanoag Tribes, 83, 103
Warner, John, 29
Warner, Mark, 29, 81, 84
Washington, 38
Washington, D.C., 98
The Washington Post, 46, 64–65, 79, 83
Watkins, Arthur, 23
Wheeler–Howard Act, 21
Wind River News, 89, 92, 126
Wolf, Frank R., 79

Xolon Salinan, xv, 95

Yselta del Sur Pueblo, 108

About the Author

Cristina L. Azocar, PhD is a citizen of the Upper Mattaponi Tribe. She is a professor of journalism at San Francisco State University and serves as the faculty advisor to the Student Kouncil of Intertribal Nations (SKINS). Her research focuses on the intersection of race and journalistic practice, particularly in the area of news coverage of Indigenous people.

Azocar earned her doctorate in communication studies at the University of Michigan. She has a master's degree in ethnic studies and a bachelor's degree in journalism, both from SF State. Her interest in diversity in the news media spans more than thirty years, and began with her concern about negative news media representations of Indigenous people.

Dr. Azocar currently serves on the Accrediting Committee of the Accrediting Council on Education in Journalism and Mass Communication and was previously a council member. She served as a past president of the Native American Journalists Association, directed the Center for Integration and Improvement of Journalism for ten years, was a former editor of American Indian Issues for the Media Diversity Forum, and was an inaugural board member of the Women's Media Center. She was the first recipient of the Association for Education in Journalism and Mass Communication's Dr. Paula M. Poindexter Research Grant for research that led to this book.

Her work is published in *American Indian Quarterly, Howard Journal of Communications, Health Communication, Journal of Broadcasting and Electronic Media, Journal of Communication, Journalism and Mass Communication Educator, International Journal of Home Economics, Family & Consumer Sciences Research Journal, Communication Booknotes Quarterly, the Encyclopedia of Journalism, COVID Communication Case Studies, Struggles, Strategies and Scholarship of Teaching Race*, and *The Diversity Style Guide: A Journalist's Handbook*.

She is currently working on *Decolonizing Communication Research*, an edited book that seeks to transform the field of U.S. communication research by introducing decolonizing methodologies and theories to the discipline of mass communication.